Collins

11+
Activity & Puzzle Book

for ages 8-9

Chris Pearse, Phil Marchant
and Gemma Taylor

The authors and publisher are grateful to the copyright holders for permission to use quoted materials and images.

Published by Collins
An imprint of HarperCollinsPublishers
1 London Bridge Street
London SE1 9GF

HarperCollinsPublishers
1st Floor, Watermarque Building,
Ringsend Road, Dublin 4, Ireland

ISBN: 978-0-00-851859-2

First published 2022

10 9 8 7 6 5 4 3 2 1

©HarperCollinsPublishers Ltd. 2022

British Library Cataloguing in Publication Data.

A CIP record of this book is available from the British Library.

Publisher: Clare Souza
Authors: Chris Pearse, Phil Marchant and Gemma Taylor
Project Management and Editorial: Richard Toms and Sundus Pasha
Cover Design: Sarah Duxbury
Inside Concept Design: Ian Wrigley
Typesetting and artwork: Jouve India Private Limited
Production: Karen Nulty
Printed and bound in the UK using 100%
Renewable Electricity at CPI Group (UK) Ltd

MIX
Paper from
responsible sources
FSC www.fsc.org **FSC™ C007454**

This book is produced from independently certified FSC™ paper to ensure responsible forest management.

For more information visit:
www.harpercollins.co.uk/green

Contents

Introduction

Welcome to this 11+ Activity and Puzzle book! It has been written to help introduce 8 and 9-year-old children to the key skills needed for the 11+ tests. All the main topics are covered, including English, Maths, Verbal Reasoning and Non-Verbal Reasoning.

The main aim of the book is to make learning fun and engaging. If your child is just starting out on their 11+ journey, this is the perfect resource to build an awareness of the skills required, while enjoying the various puzzles and activities.

You can use this book to help introduce the different 11+ question types and begin to develop your child's skills. Children can work through the topics with a friend or a parent, or on their own. Try to discuss the activities they have attempted.

Children are more likely to remember the skills and enjoy the learning if the activities are approached in short bursts rather than long periods, which could make them feel tired.

Your child will be able to write some of their answers in the book, but for some questions they will need separate sheets of paper.

This book has been published in collaboration with Teachitright, one of the most successful 11+ tuition companies in the South-East. It has supported thousands of pupils for both grammar school and independent school entry. Teachitright has several tuition centres across the UK, including Berkshire, Buckinghamshire and West Midlands.

For more information, visit **www.teachitright.com**

Features of this book

Each double page spread focuses on a different question type or topic for English, Maths, Verbal Reasoning or Non-Verbal Reasoning, offering a series of activities to try. An introduction explains what skills are involved.

A **Worked example** gives children a good understanding of the style of questions posed in an actual 11+ test.

To further engage your child with the topics, **Fun facts** provide interesting pieces of related information that they could share with others.

A series of **Challenges** for each topic so that children can practise the necessary skills. These enjoyable activities are pitched at an appropriate level for 8 and 9-year-olds but are designed to develop the skills required for the 11+.

A final **Push yourself** activity extends the level of challenge a little further.

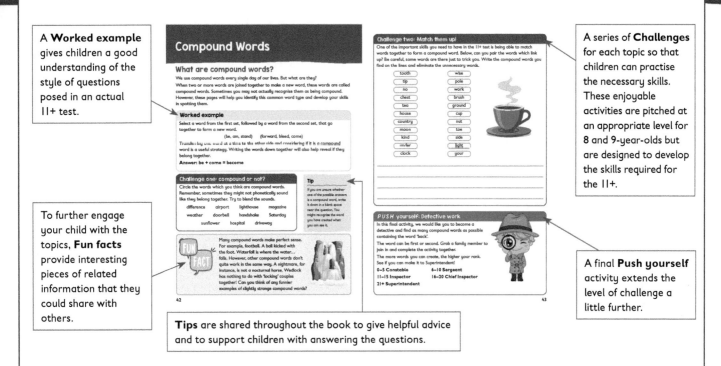

Tips are shared throughout the book to give helpful advice and to support children with answering the questions.

At the end of the English, Maths, Verbal Reasoning and Non-Verbal Reasoning sections, a Mixed Activities section rounds up your child's learning with an assortment of questions for the topics covered in the book.

Answers are provided at the back of the book to allow parents or carers to mark the questions set in the activities.

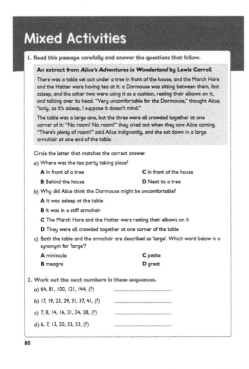

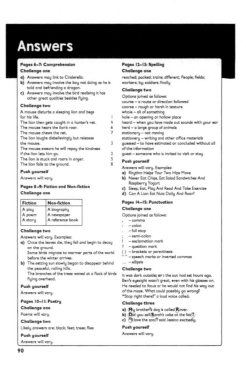

Comprehension

What is English comprehension?

We read words and sentences every day, but do we always understand what we have read? English comprehension is the ability to understand and interpret what you read. To do this, you need to:

- create mental images of a text
- think of and ask questions
- make links between what you read and what you already know
- re-read for clarity
- summarise a text in your own words
- make predictions about what will happen next.

Tip

If you are unsure of the correct answer, eliminate any options you know to be incorrect. This will narrow down the possibilities and give you a better chance of getting the answer right if you have to guess.

Worked example

Read this passage carefully and answer the question that follows.

Rose-coloured light seeped into the room. Rubbing her bleary eyes, Sara walked to the window and peeked through the narrow slats. Outside, the city streets were already a flurry of activity.

What does the rose-coloured light suggest? Circle the letter for the correct answer.

A That the sun is setting   **B** That the sun is rising

C That Sara's window is beside a street light   **D** That Sara should go back to bed

The rose-coloured light suggests it is either sunrise or sunset. From Sara rubbing her eyes and the use of the word 'already' to describe the activity in the street, we can infer that it is early morning and therefore the correct answer is **B**.

Challenge one: Making predictions

You are often asked to predict what might happen next in a story. You can develop this skill by reading books from different genres. What might happen next in these stories?

a) A girl is mistreated by her family

*I think that*_____

b) A boy is warned to stay away from dragons

*I think that*_____

c) A penguin longs to fly like the birds it sees in the sky

*I think that*_____

Challenge two: Recognising sequences

Understanding the sequence of events in a story is an important comprehension skill. Many stories follow similar themes and we can use what happened in one story to help us piece together what might happen in another.

This story has been split into its key events and jumbled up. Can you number each event so that the story makes sense?

A mouse disturbs a sleeping lion and begs for his life. ☐

The lion then gets caught in a hunter's net. ☐

The mouse hears the lion's roar. ☐

The mouse chews the net. ☐

The lion laughs disbelievingly but releases the mouse. ☐

The mouse swears he will repay the kindness if the lion lets him go. ☐

The lion is stuck and roars in anger. ☐

The lion falls to the ground. ☐

Did you know that if you read 20 minutes each day, you will read approximately 1,800,000 words per year?

PUSH yourself: Roll and respond

In this final activity, put all your English comprehension skills to use and play a game of 'roll and respond'. Grab a die and your most recent read – even if you haven't finished it yet!

What is the setting of your story? Describe it. Use specific details from the text.

Pretend you are interviewing one of the characters in the story. What two questions would you ask them and what might their answers be?

Summarise the last chapter that you read. What were the most important events? Did you learn anything new about the characters?

Find an example of a great word the author has used. What does the word mean? Look it up in a dictionary if you are unsure.

What is the book you are reading mainly about? How do you know?

What do you think will happen next? Why do you think that?

Fiction and Non-fiction

What is fiction and what is non-fiction?

A work of **fiction** is a deliberately made-up text – something told or written that is not fact. A **non-fiction** text refers to facts and is based on real people and true events.

Challenge one: Fiction or Non-fiction?

In preparation for your 11+ exam, you will need to read a variety of text types and genres to develop your reading comprehension skills and to grow your vocabulary. Can you tell the difference between a fiction and non-fiction text? Sort the texts listed below into the correct column of the table.

A play   A biography   A story

A poem   A newspaper   A reference book

Fiction	Non-fiction

The Latin word 'fictus' means 'to form'. This seems like a good origin for the English word 'fiction' since fiction is formed in the imagination!

Challenge two: Autumnal scene

a) Can you write two sentences about what you can **see** in this image as if it were a **non-fiction** text? Remember, these should be facts!

For example: *The leaves of some trees turn brown in autumn.*

_____

_____

_____

_____

b) Can you write two sentences about what you can see in this image as if it were a **fiction** text? Fiction is effectively storytelling so remember to include lots of description!

For example: *Crisp orange and yellow leaves fell gracefully from the trees, blanketing the soft, wet ground with colour.*

_____

_____

_____

_____

PUSH yourself: Book detective

In this final activity, become a 'detective' and go in search of fiction and non-fiction books around your home. Do you think your family will own more fiction or non-fiction books?

Which kind of book do you find more of? How about books belonging to your parents? Is there a reason why they might own more of one type of book than another?

Poetry

What is poetry?

A poem is a piece of writing that often uses literary devices, rhyme, rhythm or repetition to share an idea, a feeling or a story with the reader.

Challenge one: Repetition

Repetition is when a word or line is repeated several times. It helps to make the main idea of a poem more memorable. For example:

Car Sick

I'm car sick
> open a window.

I'm car sick
> take a pill.

I'm car sick
> try to sleep.

I'm car sick
> sit still.

Now it's your turn. Can you write a short poem in this same style, where one line is repeated throughout? It doesn't have to rhyme. Your poem should be titled 'I'm hungry' and you can write it on the lines here.

_____

_____

_____

_____

_____

_____

_____

_____

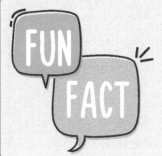

Haikus are commonly known to be some of the shortest poems. But did you know that the longest poem in the world is the Mahabharata? This is an Indian epic poem dating from the 4th century BC or earlier and it has about 1.8 million words!

Challenge two: Rhyme

Words that rhyme have the same end sound but are not always spelt the same. Poems often use pairs of words that rhyme to create a rhythm or beat which makes them easier to read. Can you fill in each of the spaces in this poem so that the missing word rhymes with the word at the end of the line above?

Zebra has fur with stripes that are black,

A long, soft muzzle; a striped mane on his _____.

Tall thin legs, a stripey tail on his seat,

A unique pattern and hooves on his _____.

Giraffe is tall with knobbly knees,

A strong, powerful neck for reaching food in the _____.

A brown patterned coat; small ears, horns and eyes

And a long fringed tail to swat away _____.

PUSH yourself: Roll and write

In this activity, you need a pair of dice and your imagination! We are going to create a poem, focusing on syllables and rhythm, by rolling the dice.

Roll the pair of dice and count up the total. You then have to write a line of poetry with that number of syllables.

For example:

I have rolled a total of 7. That means I need a phrase for my poem with just seven syllables. That won't be a very long line and that is okay! Here's one for my poem about the seaside:

Gen-tle waves kiss-ing my toes

Stuck on what to write about? Why not write about your favourite season or place to visit?

Spelling

Why is spelling important?

Spelling and reading skills are closely related and help to develop your overall literacy. Learning common spelling patterns and expanding your vocabulary is essential for success in the 11+ test.

Worked example

Complete the word on the right so that it means the opposite, or nearly the opposite, of the word on the left. Be sure to spell the word correctly.

love   l_ _ _ he

This question type requires a vast knowledge of antonyms (words with opposite meanings). This is not the only skill at play however, as your word recognition and the ability to spell tricky words comes in too. In this question, the opposite of 'love' is 'hate' but since that would not fit with the letters provided, you would need to find another word with the same meaning as 'hate'. The answer is **loathe**. See page 46 for more about antonyms.

Challenge one: Be the teacher!

In the passage below, there are 10 spelling mistakes. Find the words that are spelt wrongly and write the correct spellings in the spaces below.

When they reeched France they were pakked into trians, which

_____

stopped and started and crawled all day along the overcrowded

_____

tracks. The country didn't look so diferent. Pepole worked the

_____

feilds just as the lads had done back home. Some of the workeers

_____

unbent their backs and waved as the trains went bye. The

_____

solidiers finaly arrived at a small station that had grown into a

_____

vast supply depot.

_____

Did you know that you can spell out all of the numbers from 1 to 99 without using the letter A?

Challenge two: Homophones!

Homophones are words that sound the same but have different spellings and meanings. These can be tricky to learn and understand.

Here is a list of homophones. Draw lines to join each word to its correct meaning.

course	all of something
coarse	to have estimated or concluded without all of the information
whole	when you have made out sounds with your ear
hole	not moving
heard	a large group of animals
herd	someone who is invited to visit or stay
stationary	writing and other office materials
stationery	an opening or hollow place
guessed	a route or direction followed
guest	rough or harsh in texture

PUSH yourself: Make some mnemonics

A mnemonic is a tool that can help you to learn tricky spellings. You take each of the letters in a word and make a phrase. Each word of the phrase begins with the letters that spell that tricky word. For example:

B-E-C-A-U-S-E   Big Elephants Can Always Understand Small Elephants

Make a mnemonic for each of these spellings.

a) R-H-Y-T-H-M

_____

b) N-E-C-E-S-S-A-R-Y

_____

c) S-E-P-A-R-A-T-E

_____

d) C-A-L-E-N-D-A-R

_____

Punctuation

What is punctuation?

Punctuation is a set of specific symbols used to show the meaning of a sentence and how it should be read. There are 14 punctuation marks that are commonly used in the English language.

Worked example

In which of the following sentences has a comma been incorrectly used or left out?

A After the war, bright red poppies grew on the field.

B Soldiers, who had travelled from great distances, slowly returned to their homes.

C The nurses treated patients with bruises bumps and breaks.

D Even though he had been injured, the soldier continued to fight.

This question is testing your knowledge of commas and their many uses. Option A shows a comma following a fronted adverbial and D demonstrates a comma used to separate a main clause from a subordinate clause. B is an example of a relative clause, where the commas bracket the additional information placed in the middle of the sentence.

C is the answer because commas need to be used in a list:

The nurses treated patients with bruises, bumps and breaks.

Challenge one: Match them up!

Draw lines to match each symbol to its correct name.

,	question mark
:	comma
.	colon
'	speech marks or inverted commas
;	full stop
!	semi-colon
?	ellipsis
( )	brackets or parenthesis
" "	exclamation mark
...	apostrophe

Challenge two: Where do I go?

Can you place the correct punctuation in these sentences?

It was dark outside◯ the sun had set hours ago. Ben◯s eyesight

wasn't great, even with his glasses on. He needed to focus or he would not find his

way out of the maze. What could possibly go wrong◯

◯Stop right there◯" a loud voice called◯

In the UK, we may call it an 'at' symbol or 'at' mark. However, in the Netherlands it is called a 'monkey's tail', in Italy it is known as a 'small snail', and in Russia it is called a 'little dog'!

Challenge three: Spot the mistakes!

Each of the following sentences contains three punctuation mistakes. These mistakes might simply be that a form of punctuation is missing or that the incorrect piece of punctuation has been used. Write the sentences with the punctuation corrected.

a) my brothers dog is called rover. _____

b) did you sell sarah's cake at the fair. _____

c) i love the zoo, said Jessica excitedly. _____

PUSH yourself: Punctuation search

Choose a page of your latest reading book and go on a punctuation search! See how many of the punctuation marks listed in the table below you can find on that page. Each piece of punctuation has a different value.
How many points can you score?

? ! . Capital letters	1 point
, ' " "	2 points
: ;	3 points
( ) ... –	4 points

Grammar

What do we mean by grammar?

Grammar is the set of rules we follow when creating sentences as we speak or write. Grammar is the first step towards good communication, reading comprehension and writing, so it is important to develop your skills in this area.

Worked example

Find the adjective in the sentence below.

She had the peculiar habit of playing the piano whenever there was a storm on the horizon.

A she   **B** horizon   **C** peculiar   **D** playing

This question relies on you knowing the different word types. An adjective is a word that describes a noun. The only adjective in this sentence is 'peculiar' and therefore the answer is **C**.

Challenge one: Tense times

There are three main tenses: present, past and future. The tense you are writing in often affects the form of the verb you are using. For example:

Present tense: I jump / I am jumping

Past tense: I jumped / I have jumped

Future tense: I will jump

Read each of the sentences below. They are currently in the present tense. Change the sentences to the past tense by starting them with 'Yesterday, I…'.

a) I am buying my lunch at the shop.

Yesterday, I _____

b) Right now, I am writing in my diary.

_____

c) Just now, I am drinking my juice.

_____

d) Currently, I am swimming lengths in the pool.

_____

e) At present, I am teaching my friend to play chess.

_____

Challenge two: Get colouring!

Four of the main word types in the English language are:

Nouns	A person, place or object
Verbs	A word used to describe an action, state or occurrence
Adjectives	A word that describes a noun
Adverbs	A word that describes a verb; it tells you how something is done

Grab your coloured pens and use a different colour for each word type. Can you pick out the nouns, verbs, adjectives and adverbs in the sentences below? There may be more than one example of each per sentence. If you get stuck, see page 19 for examples of nouns, verbs, adjectives and adverbs.

a) The sleepy cat purred loudly as the young boy stroked it.

b) It lazily rose to its feet and rubbed up against the attentive boy.

c) Eventually, the black cat stalked off slowly to see if it was time for dinner.

PUSH yourself: Word play

In this final activity, you will need another family member or two! Using the lists below, select one verb and one adverb to act out to your audience. Whoever guesses the words you are performing gets a point and takes the next turn at acting.

Verbs

Gobbling	Whistling	Sprinting	Falling	Stretching
Dancing	Skiing	Whispering	Crying	Painting

Adverbs

Quietly	Hungrily	Gracefully	Carefully	Excitedly
Painfully	Loudly	Angrily	Dreamily	Cheerfully

Once you have used all of these words, why not add some of your own? This game is endless!

A sentence which contains all 26 letters of the English alphabet is called a pangram. A famous pangram is 'The quick brown fox jumps over the lazy dog'. Can you create your own pangram?

Word Groups

What are word groups?

In the previous topic, we looked at grammar and the four main word types: nouns, verbs, adjectives and adverbs. Whilst these are the four main word types used in the English language, there are other word groups needed to create full and complex sentences. These include:

Conjunctions	Words that join phrases, clauses or sentences
Articles	A word that introduces a noun
Prepositions	Words that usually go in front of a noun and describe the position of it
Pronouns	Words that take the place of nouns

Worked example

Insert the best articles to fill the spaces in the sentence below.

I went to _____ market to buy _____ punnet of strawberries.

*Answer: I went to **the** market to buy **a** punnet of strawberries.*

The most common articles are 'a', 'an' and 'the', and these provide further detail about the noun that follows. In this sentence, I was familiar with 'the market' and therefore 'the' was a more suitable article than 'a'. Equally, I did not go to the market for a specific punnet of strawberries and therefore 'a' was the correct article for this noun.

Challenge one: Word sorting

Sort the following words into their correct groups: nouns, verbs, adjectives or adverbs.

frozen	fair	crossly	bookcase	malicious	sprinting
deliberately	octopus	hurrying	sometimes	sweeping	umbrella

Nouns	Verbs	Adjectives	Adverbs

18

Challenge two: Brain buster

Now that you are more familiar with the different word types, see if you can come up with a few examples of each on your own.

For each word type, write two examples. One example has already been given for you.

Word type	Example words
Articles	the, ,
Nouns	chair, ,
Pronouns	he, ,
Adjectives	spotty, ,
Verbs	chased, ,
Adverbs	perfectly, ,
Conjunctions	and, ,
Prepositions	under, ,

Tip

If you are finding it tricky to think of a conjunction, the acronym 'FANBOYS' might be a useful one for you to learn! Each letter represents a conjunction commonly used to join two equally important ideas:

For **A**nd **N**or **B**ut **O**r **Y**et **S**o

PUSH yourself: Silly sentences

Here is a twist on a classic game you may have played before. You will need a piece of paper and someone to play with. At the top of the page, you will be asked to write something (e.g. an article and an adjective) and then fold it over backwards. Then, you pass that piece of paper to the next person and they are asked to write something different (e.g. a noun). They fold their writing backwards and hand the paper back to you, where you will be asked to write something else. Play continues until a complete sentence has been written containing lots of different word types.

Here is an example of the word types you might use and a sentence in that order:

Article and adjective	A cheeky
Noun	mouse
Verb	scurried
Adverb	cautiously
Preposition	through
Article and adjective	the narrow
Noun	hole

What silly sentences might you come up with?

Did you know a new word is added to the dictionary every two hours? This means that in the time it takes your parents to tell you a word you are using is 'not real', somewhere else in the world that very word may be being added to a dictionary!

Literary Devices

What are literary devices?

Literary devices are tools used by an author to enhance writing and to make reading more interesting. Here are some commonly used literary devices:

- alliteration

- onomatopoeia

- personification

- similes (a comparison between two things containing the word 'like' or 'as')

- metaphors (a comparison between two things containing the word 'is')

- hyperbole or exaggeration

Worked example

'The car burned like the blazing sun and a fire crew was quick to arrive.'

What literary device is this an example of?

A metaphor   **B** simile   **C** personification   **D** onomatopoeia

This question is testing your knowledge of literary devices. In this case, the word 'like' in the quote reveals that a simile has been used to compare the car to the sun. Therefore, the answer is **B**.

Challenge one: Onomatopoeia

Onomatopoeia is a type of word that sounds like what it describes, for example 'boom' and 'meow'. Can you write a word to describe the sound associated with each of these pictures?

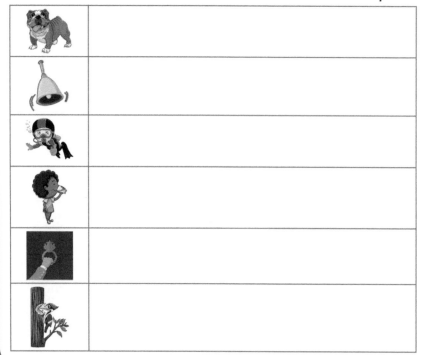

Do you remember learning 'Old MacDonald had a Farm' as a child? This song associates an animal with the sound it makes – meaning that you probably learned onomatopoeia before you even learned how to speak properly!

Challenge two: Personification

Personification is when you describe objects by giving them human feelings or actions.

a) Can you underline what is being personified in the following sentences?

   i) The street lights glared at me wickedly in the dark night.

   ii) Snowflakes danced around me like little white ballerinas.

   iii) The tree reached its gnarled fingers toward me.

   iv) The daffodils swayed melodically in the spring breeze.

b) Now it's your turn! Pair each of these objects with one of the verbs listed below and write your own examples of personification.

| **Objects:** | sun | alarm clock | thunder | leaves | moon |
| **Verbs:** | smiled | roared | stretched | screamed | refused |

_____

_____

_____

_____

_____

PUSH yourself: Alliteration

Alliteration is the technique of using two or more words together which begin with the same letter or sound. In this final activity, try to write an alliterative poem. On a piece of paper, write the numbers one to ten down the side of your page in words. Each of these numbers begins with a different sound and it is your job to write an alliterative sentence for each one.

Here is the first line to get you started! The sounds have also been listed for you.

/w/	One waggly walrus wore a wet welly
/t/	Two…
/th/ or /f/	Three…
/f/ or /th/	Four…
/f/ or /th/	Five…
/s/	Six…
/s/	Seven…
/ā/ Long a sound: a, a_e, ay, ai, ey, ei	Eight…
/n/	Nine…
/t/	Ten…

Cloze

What is cloze?

A cloze test is a way of checking your understanding of a text by removing words. There are three main types of cloze: multiple choice, partial letter and word bank.

Tip

It is always useful to read past the gaps to gain a greater understanding of what the sentence, or whole text, is about.

Challenge one: Multiple choice cloze

Read the passage and select one of the options to fill each of the gaps labelled A, B, C and D.

An extract from *Peter Pan* by J. M. Barrie

All children, except one, grow up. They __A__ know that they will grow up, and the way Wendy knew was this. One day when she was two years old, she was playing in a __B__ , and she plucked another flower and ran with it to her mother. I suppose she must have looked rather __C__, for Mrs. Darling put her hand to her heart and cried, "Oh, why can't you remain like this for ever!" This was all that passed between them on the subject, but henceforth Wendy knew that she must grow up. You always know after you are two. Two is the beginning of the __D__.

A	never	soon	don't
B	bedroom	sandpit	garden
C	delightful	awful	miserable
D	future	day	end

Challenge two: Partial letter cloze

Fill in the missing letters in the five incomplete words in the passage below.

An extract from *Grimms' Fairy Tales* by Jacob and Wilhelm Grimm

Rapunzel grew into the most **b_ _ _ _ _ful** child under the sun. When she was twelve years old, the enchantress shut her into a tower, which lay in a **f_ _ _st**, and had neither stairs nor door, but quite at the top was a little **w_ _ d _w**. When the enchantress wanted to go in, she placed herself beneath it and cried:

'Rapunzel, Rapunzel, Let down your **h_ _ r** to me.'

Rapunzel had magnificent long hair, fine as spun gold, and when she heard the voice of the enchantress she unfastened her braided tresses, wound them round one of the hooks of the window above, and then the hair fell twenty ells down, and the enchantress **cli_ _ _d** up by it.

PUSH yourself: Word bank cloze

A 'word bank cloze' is simply a text taken from a book where some of the words have been removed and placed in a word bank for you to choose from. In preparation for the 11+ test, you might complete lots of cloze activities and they could be passages taken from classical books you may not have read.

In this final activity, you will need to ask a family member to help. Find one of your favourite books, or even just a book you have read recently, and ask them to write up one of the pages whilst leaving out certain words. They need to place all the words they have removed in a word bank so that you can use it to complete the cloze later.

See how you find completing a cloze exercise when you know the story. Does it make it easier?

Understanding Number

How well do you know your numbers?

In the 11+ test, having a good grasp of number skills and the four operations is fundamental. Knowing the value of digits helps you to read, write and order numbers.

Worked example

What is the value of the 7 in the following number?

13,7̲90.548

Read the number as it appears and this will help reveal the value of the 7.

Thirteen thousand, **seven hundred** and ninety, and five hundred and forty-eight thousandths.

Being able to understand the value of numbers will support adding and subtracting figures correctly.

Challenge one: Magic square

Place the numbers 1 to 8 in each square of the grid, so that each side adds up to the middle number.

	12	

Tip

Basic arithmetic helps in other areas of mathematics, such as percentages, ratio or even algebra.

Did you know there are different names for the number '0'? These include zero, nought, naught, nil, zilch and zip. Another interesting fact are the numbers which come after a million, billion and trillion. Can you find them out?

Challenge two: Special numbers

In this exercise, you are going to explore special numbers. These include prime, square, cube and triangular numbers. Using the number square below, circle the various special numbers using the colour coding given. Beware that some numbers will fit into more than one category of special number.

Prime numbers: blue
Square numbers: green
Cube numbers: red
Triangular numbers: black

Remember:

A **prime number** is a special number greater than 1 that has exactly two factors: itself and 1.

A **square number** is the result of multiplying a number by itself.

A **cube number** is the result of multiplying a number by itself and multiplying it by itself again.

A **triangular number** is a number that can be shown by a pattern of dots arranged in an equilateral triangle with the same number of dots on each side.

1	2	3	4	5	6	7	8	9	10
11	12	13	14	15	16	17	18	19	20
21	22	23	24	25	26	27	28	29	30
31	32	33	34	35	36	37	38	39	40
41	42	43	44	45	46	47	48	49	50
51	52	53	54	55	56	57	58	59	60
61	62	63	64	65	66	67	68	69	70
71	72	73	74	75	76	77	78	79	80
81	82	83	84	85	86	87	88	89	90
91	92	93	94	95	96	97	98	99	100

Did you find any numbers which appear in more than one category?

PUSH yourself: Balloon bursting

This activity will help you test those number identifying skills. If a number in one of the balloons is included in the answers to the three operations below, then that balloon will burst.

1. Balloons with a multiple of 9
2. Square number balloons
3. Prime number balloons

Which balloon number are you left with?

Tip

Learning your times tables off by heart is a vital skill for the 11+ test. If you don't know them yet, make sure you practise them at home.

Time

Are you right on time?

Make sure you have a good understanding of time. In the 11+ test, you might have to answer questions about bus or train timetables or find the difference between times. You will need to work in the 12- or 24-hour clock format.

Worked example

Anya goes to an after-school sports session starting at 15:30. The session is 1 hour and 10 minutes long. If it takes her 12 minutes to walk home afterwards, at what time will she arrive home?

There are some key facts involved when solving time questions:

- 60 seconds in a minute
- 60 minutes in an hour
- 24 hours in a day.

In this example, adding the time in separate intervals is a logical approach.

15:30 (1 hour) 16:30 (10 minutes) 16:40 (12 minutes) **16:52**

Challenge one: Good timing

Questions in the 11+ test may use the 12- or 24-hour clock. The 12-hour clock runs from 12 midnight to 12 noon (am times) and then from 12 noon to 12 midnight (pm times). The 24-hour clock uses the numbers 00:00 to 23:59 (midnight is 00:00).

Draw lines from a time in the first column to the matching time in the second column.

17:00	2 pm
19:00	11 pm
23:00	3 am
08:00	7 pm
21:00	5 pm
13:00	8 am
03:00	1 pm
14:00	9 pm

Challenge two: Reading a timetable

Being able to read a timetable is a useful life skill. Timetables help to show how long your journey will take and at what time you will arrive at your destination.

Look carefully at the train timetable below and answer the questions that follow.

	Train 1	Train 2	Train 3	Train 4	Train 5	Train 6
Broad Street	06:50		07:25	08:45	09:10	09:45
Longbrook	07:00	07:25	07:41	08:55	09:19	09:53
Stonebridge	07:11	07:41	07:51	09:04	09:31	10:02
New Cross	07:18	07:59	07:59	09:11	09:38	10:11
Green Field	07:29	08:12	08:09	09:16	09:47	10:16
South Manor	07:33	08:15	08:14	09:20	09:53	10:21
Uplands Park	07:45	08:30	08:30		10:05	10:40

a) How long is the journey from Green Field to Uplands Park on train 3? _____

b) If you take the fifth train from New Cross, how many
   minutes does the journey take to South Manor? _____

c) Which train is the fastest if you travel from Green Field to South Manor? _____

PUSH yourself: Time quiz

Have a go at these quiz-style questions and put your time knowledge to the test.

a) How many hours are in 3 days? _____

b) How many months of the year have 31 days? _____

c) How many seconds are in 10 minutes? _____

d) How many years are in a decade? _____

e) How many minutes are in 2 hours? _____

FUN FACT

You can use the knuckles of your hand to remember which months have 31 days. Count knuckles as months with 31 days and spaces between the knuckles as months with 30 or fewer days.

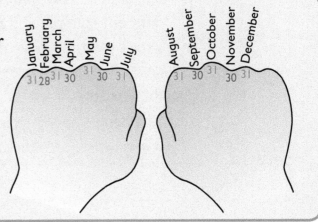

Area and Perimeter

What do these words mean?

The **area** is the 'space inside' or the surface that a 2D shape covers.

The **perimeter** is the distance around the outside edge of a 2D shape.

When solving area and perimeter problems, you could be working with different units of measurement. These include millimetres (mm), centimetres (cm), metres (m) or kilometres (km).

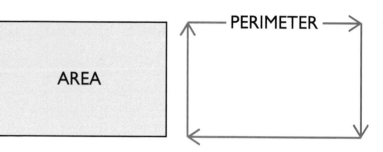

AREA

PERIMETER

Worked example

Look carefully at this shape and calculate its perimeter and its area.

Calculating the perimeter:

Add together all the lengths. As this is a rectangle, you know the opposite sides are the same length. Therefore, adding together 3 cm + 8 cm + 3 cm + 8 cm gives a perimeter of **22 cm**.

3 cm

8 cm

Calculating the area:

Multiply the length by the width. This can be written as L × W = Area.

In this example, the area is 3 cm × 8 cm = **24 cm²**. The small '2' means 'squared'.

True or false?

Can you prove or disprove the statement below? Grab some squared paper and draw yourself some different squares and rectangles. Work out their perimeters and areas. Check the answers against the statement.

'The perimeter for squares and rectangles is always less than their area.'

Tip

To help remember what the perimeter is, imagine an ant crawling around the outside of the shape and not being able to enter inside.

Challenge one: Working with shapes

Work out the perimeter and the area of each shape. Each grid square is 1 cm².

a) Perimeter = _____   Area = _____

b) Perimeter = _____   Area = _____

c) Perimeter = _____   Area = _____

d) Perimeter = _____   Area = _____

e) Perimeter = _____   Area = _____

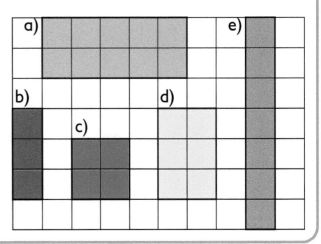

Challenge two: Equivalent values

You need to know equivalent values for perimeter and area problems. A question might use one unit of measurement, while the answer options use another. In this activity, draw lines to join pairs of ovals that show equivalent lengths.

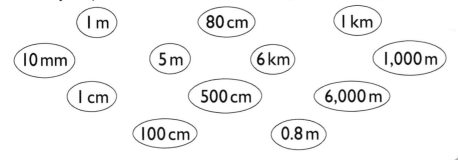

Tip

When calculating the perimeter of a compound shape, be careful not to count a side twice. Put a line or mark on the side you start with, so you know when you have got back to the start.

PUSH yourself: Compound shapes

A compound shape is made up of several simpler shapes. In this example, you are not provided with all the lengths. However, you can use the given measurements to work out the missing numbers. For example, the top length can be worked out as 7 cm by adding the 2 cm at the bottom with the 5 cm horizontal line.

What is the perimeter of this compound shape?   _____

1 cm

5 cm

4 cm

2 cm

To calculate the area of compound shapes, you can break them down into individual rectangles. Once you have divided the shape into smaller rectangles, you can multiply the length by the width for each of them. Don't forget to add the amounts together to find the overall area of the compound shape.

What is the area of this compound shape?   _____

2D and 3D Shapes

Do you shape up well?

In our everyday lives we see objects around us that have different shapes. These shapes can be either 2D (two-dimensional) or 3D (three-dimensional).

An example of an everyday 2D shape would be a sheet of paper as it only has a length and a width (it is flat!). However, a box has a length, a width and a height, and so is 3D.

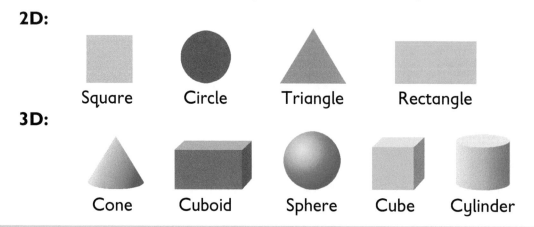

2D:
Square   Circle   Triangle   Rectangle

3D:
Cone   Cuboid   Sphere   Cube   Cylinder

Worked example

Which shape below is a regular pentagon? Circle your answer.

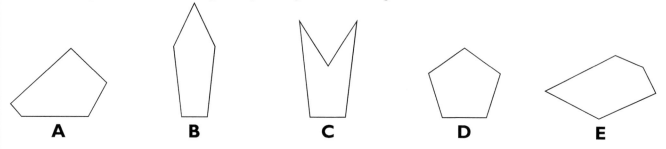

A   B   C   D   E

A polygon that is five-sided is called a pentagon. The question above also tests your understanding of the words **regular** and **irregular**. A regular pentagon is one in which all the sides and angles are equal; otherwise it would be irregular. The answer is **D**.

Challenge one: Shape and space quiz

To know about shapes, you need to know specific facts. Test your knowledge here.

a) What 2D shape has eight sides? _____

b) How many sides does a hexagon have? _____

c) How many triangular faces does a square pyramid have? _____

d) What shape is the base of a cylinder? _____

e) How many square faces does a cube have? _____

Challenge two: Parts of a circle

In the 11+ test, you might be asked questions relating to circles. Here is a diagram that shows all the different parts of a circle.

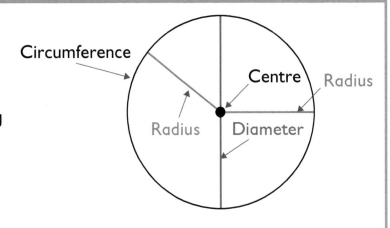

A typical question might involve solving the radius and diameter of a circle.

The **radius** is the distance from the centre to the edge of the circle. The radius is half the circle's diameter.

The outer edge of the circle is called the **circumference**.

The **diameter** is the distance from one part of the circumference to the other, passing through the centre of the circle.

Now try this question.

Jaspreet and her family have ordered three large pizzas. The radius of one pizza is 15 cm. If all the pizzas were arranged in a line, how many centimetres long would it be? _____

PUSH yourself: Guess the shape

This topic has already demonstrated there is quite a bit of vocabulary to learn when studying 2D and 3D shapes. The following activity will really get you thinking about the key words associated with shape and space. Below are a series of clues to a shape. Can you guess the shape correctly in as few clues as possible? The fewer the clues, the more marks!

1. I am a four-sided shape. (5 marks)

2. I have one pair of parallel sides. (4 marks)

3. The sum of my angles is 360°. (3 marks)

4. Not all my sides are equal in length. (2 marks)

5. I look like a car windscreen. (1 mark)

    What am I? _____

The study of shapes and space is called 'geometry'. This word comes from the ancient Greek and means 'measuring the Earth'. Geometry is very useful in everyday life and for that reason it was developed much earlier than other areas of maths.

Tip

Create a glossary of terms for shape and space using all the key words you can find on this topic.

Percentages

What are percentages?

Percentages might be a maths topic that you haven't learnt at school – yet! – but here we will gently introduce them. The word **percent** means 'out of 100'.

Have you ever seen percentage signs before? If you've been shopping or just looked through a shop window, you might have noticed signs like these.

Percentages are often used for discounts on products. There is one percentage sign you will never see in a shop window – that is 100% off because this would mean that everything in the shop is free!

Worked example

Find 30% of £50.

In percentage questions like these, it can be easier to find 10% first.

Finding 10% is simple because you just need to divide by 10.

Dividing £50 by 10 equals £5. So £5 represents 10%.

You can then multiply by 3 to find 30%.

£5 × 3 = **£15**

Challenge one: Percentages table

Try to develop your understanding of percentages by filling in the gaps in this table.

Percentage	Out of 100	How to find this percentage of an amount
1%	$\frac{1}{100}$	Divide the amount by 100
5%		Divide the amount by 20
10%	$\frac{10}{100}$	
25%		
		Divide the amount by 2
	$\frac{75}{100}$	

Challenge two: Best bargain

Can you work out which pair of trainers would be the cheaper if the different discounts are given?

White and Black Trainers
Normal price: £40

Discount: 40%

White and Red Trainers
Normal price: £30

Discount: 30%

PUSH yourself: Solve the survey problem

Andrew did a survey of 55 children at school. He wanted to see how many were left-handed.

Andrew says, '*The results show exactly 10% of the people in the survey were left-handed.*'

Why can't Andrew be correct?

How amazing!

Did you know the human body is made up of largely water? An adult's body is usually 50% to 65% water. A jellyfish is 95% water.

Tip

Linking percentages to your knowledge of factors of 100 will help you to solve these 11+ question types. For example, if you know 25 and 4 are factor pairs of 100, then 25% is actually a quarter $\left(\dfrac{1}{4}\right)$ and to work out 25% of an amount you divide by 4.

Angles

Do you know your angles?

An angle is created when two straight lines meet. Do you know these types of angles?

Acute angle	Right angle	Obtuse angle	Straight angle	Reflex angle
An angle of less than 90°	An angle of exactly 90°	An angle greater than 90° but less than 180°	An angle of exactly 180°	An angle greater than 180° but less than 360°
Acute angle — Less than 90 degrees	Right angle — Exactly 90 degrees	Obtuse angle — Greater than 90 degrees and less than 180 degrees	Straight angle — Exactly 180 degrees	Reflex angle — Greater than 180 degrees

---

Worked example

In a right-angled triangle, one angle is 62°. What is the smallest angle of the triangle?

The angles inside a triangle always total 180°.

Knowing this is vital for this question.

First, add together the two angles that you know about (the right angle of 90° and 62°).

$$90° + 62° = 152°$$

Then subtract 152° from 180° to find the size of the third angle.

$$180° − 152° = 28°$$

28° is the smallest of the three angles so this is the correct answer.

Did you know that a **perigon** is a complete turn or a full angle. If you turn through 360°, you will end up facing the same way.

'A 180-degree turn' is a phrase you might hear to mean that someone turned around and went in the opposite direction.

180°

Challenge one: Interior angles

The angles inside a triangle total 180°. In a quadrilateral, they total 360°.

There is a useful formula to find out the total of the interior angles in 2D shapes. It is:

Total of interior angles = (n – 2) × 180°

(where n is the number of sides on the 2D shape)

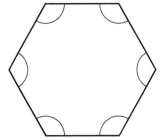

Using the formula, work out the total of the interior angles inside a hexagon. _____

Challenge two: Angles in names

Finding angles in your name can be good fun. Write your name in capital letters like the example below. Highlight all the right angles – how many are there? Which capital letter has the most right angles?

Repeat the activity with one of your friend's names. Does their name have more or fewer right angles than yours?

CLAIRE

PUSH yourself: Work out the angles

Find the angles labelled a, b and c.

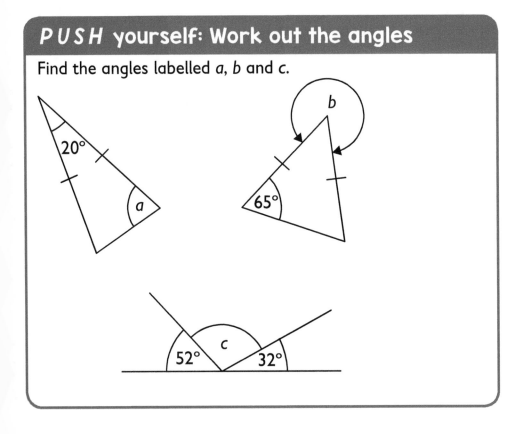

Tip

Each angle inside an equilateral triangle is 60°.

Tip

The short marks on the sides of a 2D shape (as seen on the two triangles to the left) mean that those sides are equal in length.

Data Handling

Can you deal with data?

For the 11+ test, you need to understand and work with data from a range of statistical charts and graphs. There are a variety of ways to present data, such as Venn diagrams, bar charts, line graphs, pictograms and pie charts. Some of these are shown here.

Worked example

This **pictogram** shows the number of goals scored by four football teams in one season.

Rovers

Rams

Rangers

Ravens

 Represents 10 goals

How many goals were scored altogether?

In this example, each whole football represents 10 goals. To help count the total accurately, you can write the number of goals for each team on the right. The answer is **100**.

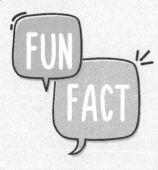

Junior scientists?

Collecting data can help to prove or disprove theories. Scientists collect data to test, change or update their theories. You could have a go at collecting the amount of rainfall or recording the daily temperature over a certain time period and then try to represent the information in a bar chart.

Challenge one: Ranking sports clubs

Pie charts show fractions of a whole and provide a clear visual representation of collected information. Remember that the angles in a pie chart will total 360° because it is a circle.

This chart shows the most popular sports clubs at a school. Can you rank the sports in order of popularity underneath, starting with the most popular?

_____   _____

_____   _____

_____   _____

_____

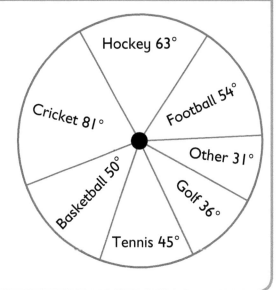

PUSH yourself: Venn diagrams

Venn diagrams are made up of overlapping circles to show two or more pieces of information that share a common feature. They can be used to classify shapes or show special numbers:

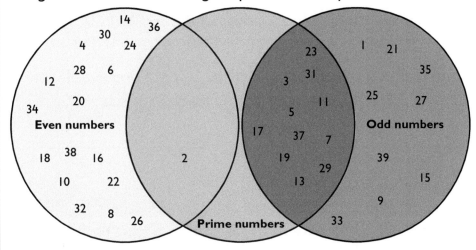

This task will really get you thinking! Use each of the digits 1 to 5 once to replace the letters A, B, C, D and E. However, the total for each circle in the Venn diagram should be equal.

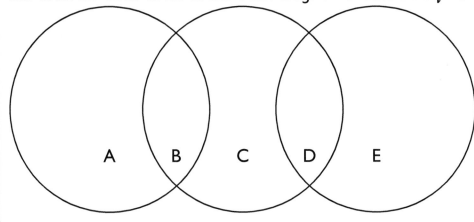

Tip

You can collect data for all sorts of different reasons, for example a survey of vehicles, hair colour or favourite hobbies. Use a chart or diagram that shows the data in the best way.

Averages

Why is the average useful?

The average helps to represent a set of data – it is a 'normal' or 'typical' value in that set of data. An example might be the average spending by supermarket customers. Each customer will spend different amounts but the average gives an idea of what the typical customer spends.

Averages can be calculated in several different ways. The most widely used type of average is the **mean**. To calculate the mean, add together all the values and divide by the number of values.

Worked example

Year 4 completed a spelling test out of 10. Here are the scores achieved by children in the Spider table group:

$$9 \quad 3 \quad 7 \quad 10 \quad 5 \quad 8$$

What was the average score for this group?

To calculate the mean for this group, you must add together all the scores:

$9 + 3 + 7 + 10 + 5 + 8 = 42$

Now, to find the average you must divide by how many scores you are presented with. In this question there are six scores. So divide the total by the number of scores:

$$42 \div 6 = \mathbf{7}$$

Challenge one: Most frequent

One of the other words to help us understand data better is **mode**. This is easily remembered by the 'mo' because it refers to the **<u>most</u>** frequent value. To find the mode (or the modal number), it is easier to reorder the data and then count how many of each value.

This table shows the number of cars that passed Faisal's house every hour.

Time	9–10 am	10–11 am	11 am – 12 noon	12 noon – 1 pm	1–2 pm	2–3 pm	3–4 pm	4–5 pm
Number of cars	7	12	8	15	8	13	6	11

What was the modal number of cars? _____

Challenge two: Middle number

Another type of 'average' is the **median**. This involves finding the value which appears in the middle of a set of data once all the values are ordered from smallest to largest.

Here are the science test scores at Cherry Lane Primary:

| 15 | 12 | 13 | 17 | 19 | 14 | 20 | 10 | 20 |

Find the median of these scores. _____

The term **average** occurs frequently in all sorts of everyday situations. For example, you might say to your friends at school, '*I'm having an average day today*', meaning that your day is neither particularly good or bad; it is about normal. We may also describe other things, like food or games, as 'average'.

Tip

If you want to calculate the median from an even number of values, you order them and then add together the two middle numbers and divide them by 2.

Challenge three: House numbers

The numbers on five houses next to each other add up to 125. What are those five numbers?

PUSH yourself: Mean puzzle

Can you solve this tricky average question? It might involve some trial and error. However, keep persevering and you will be able to work it out.

The mean of three numbers is 3. Two of the numbers are the same but the third is smaller.

What are the three numbers?

_____   _____   _____

Tip

This rhyme is a handy way to remember the different types of average:
*Hey diddle diddle,
the median's the middle;
You add and divide for the mean.
The mode is the one that appears the most,
And the range is the difference between.*

Fractions

How familiar are you with fractions?

Fractions are used to represent smaller pieces (or parts) of a whole.

 $\dfrac{4}{6}$ ← numerator
← denominator

The **numerator** is the top number of a fraction and represents how many parts you have.

The **denominator** is the bottom number of a fraction and shows how many parts make up the whole.

Worked example

What fraction of one minute is 25 seconds?

First, you need to know how many seconds there are in a minute (see pages 26–27 if you need a recap) so that both units in the question are in seconds.

60 seconds is equivalent to 1 minute.

So 25 seconds as a fraction of 1 minute is $\dfrac{25}{60}$

Although this is correct, the fraction can be changed to a simpler form using smaller numbers.

Think about the common factors of both numbers. In this example, we can divide both the numerator (25) and the denominator (60) by 5.

$$\dfrac{25}{60} \xrightarrow{\div 5} \dfrac{5}{12}$$

Challenge one: Adding fractions

You might be asked to add two fractions that have different denominators.
Try this question:

$$\dfrac{1}{2} + \dfrac{3}{7}$$

First, make the denominators the same by finding the lowest common multiple of 2 and 7, which is 14. So, you will need to convert both fractions so that they have a denominator of 14 before adding them.

$$\dfrac{1}{2} + \dfrac{3}{7} = \underline{\hspace{3cm}}$$

Challenge two: Fraction word problems

Fraction questions in the 11+ test are usually word problems rather than simply calculations. Can you solve this fraction word problem?

Two-thirds of a railing fence has been painted black.

If there are still 15 metres left to paint, how long is the railing? _____

PUSH yourself: Reordering fractions

Reorder this set of fractions from smallest to largest.

$\frac{3}{4}$ $\frac{8}{16}$ $\frac{2}{8}$ $\frac{20}{25}$ $\frac{1}{24}$

_____

Tip

A **proper** fraction has a **numerator less than the denominator**. Remember that a proper fraction is always less than 1.

An **improper** fraction has a **numerator greater than the denominator**. Therefore, an improper fraction is greater than 1.

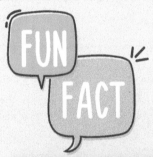

A fractions wall is a fun way to see how different fractions can be equal in value to one another. For example, can you see that $\frac{1}{3}$ is equal to $\frac{2}{6}$? See how many other pairs of equivalent fractions you can find using the wall.

1											
$\frac{1}{2}$						$\frac{1}{2}$					
$\frac{1}{3}$				$\frac{1}{3}$				$\frac{1}{3}$			
$\frac{1}{4}$			$\frac{1}{4}$			$\frac{1}{4}$			$\frac{1}{4}$		
$\frac{1}{5}$		$\frac{1}{5}$		$\frac{1}{5}$			$\frac{1}{5}$			$\frac{1}{5}$	
$\frac{1}{6}$		$\frac{1}{6}$		$\frac{1}{6}$		$\frac{1}{6}$		$\frac{1}{6}$		$\frac{1}{6}$	
$\frac{1}{7}$	$\frac{1}{7}$		$\frac{1}{7}$		$\frac{1}{7}$		$\frac{1}{7}$		$\frac{1}{7}$		$\frac{1}{7}$
$\frac{1}{8}$	$\frac{1}{8}$	$\frac{1}{8}$		$\frac{1}{8}$		$\frac{1}{8}$		$\frac{1}{8}$		$\frac{1}{8}$	$\frac{1}{8}$
$\frac{1}{9}$	$\frac{1}{9}$	$\frac{1}{9}$	$\frac{1}{9}$		$\frac{1}{9}$		$\frac{1}{9}$		$\frac{1}{9}$	$\frac{1}{9}$	$\frac{1}{9}$
$\frac{1}{10}$	$\frac{1}{10}$	$\frac{1}{10}$	$\frac{1}{10}$	$\frac{1}{10}$		$\frac{1}{10}$		$\frac{1}{10}$	$\frac{1}{10}$	$\frac{1}{10}$	$\frac{1}{10}$
$\frac{1}{11}$	$\frac{1}{11}$	$\frac{1}{11}$	$\frac{1}{11}$	$\frac{1}{11}$	$\frac{1}{11}$	$\frac{1}{11}$	$\frac{1}{11}$	$\frac{1}{11}$	$\frac{1}{11}$	$\frac{1}{11}$	$\frac{1}{11}$
$\frac{1}{12}$	$\frac{1}{12}$	$\frac{1}{12}$	$\frac{1}{12}$	$\frac{1}{12}$	$\frac{1}{12}$	$\frac{1}{12}$	$\frac{1}{12}$	$\frac{1}{12}$	$\frac{1}{12}$	$\frac{1}{12}$	$\frac{1}{12}$

Compound Words

What are compound words?

We use compound words every single day of our lives. But what are they?

When two or more words are joined together to make a new word, these words are called compound words. Sometimes you may not actually recognise them as being compound. However, these pages will help you identify this common word type and develop your skills in spotting them.

Worked example

Select a word from the first set, followed by a word from the second set, that go together to form a new word.

(be, am, stand)   (forward, bleed, come)

Transferring one word at a time to the other side and considering if it is a compound word is a useful strategy. Writing the words down together will also help reveal if they belong together.

Answer: be + come = become

Challenge one: compound or not?

Circle the words which you think are compound words. Remember, sometimes they might not phonetically sound like they belong together. Try to blend the sounds.

difference	airport	lighthouse	magazine
weather	doorbell	handshake	Saturday
	sunflower	hospital	driveway

Tip

If you are unsure whether one of the possible answers is a compound word, write it down in a blank space near the question. You might recognise the word you have created when you can see it.

Many compound words make perfect sense. For example, football. A ball kicked with the foot. Waterfall is where the water... falls. However, other compound words don't quite work in the same way. A nightmare, for instance, is not a nocturnal horse. Wedlock has nothing to do with 'locking' couples together! Can you think of any funnier examples of slightly strange compound words?

Challenge two: Match them up!

One of the important skills you need to have in the 11+ test is being able to match words together to form a compound word. Below, can you pair the words which link up? Be careful, some words are there just to trick you. Write the compound words you find on the lines and eliminate the unnecessary words.

tooth

tip

no

chest

tea

house

country

moon

kind

under

clock

wise

pole

work

brush

ground

cup

nut

toe

side

light

your

_____

_____

_____

_____

PUSH yourself: Detective work

In this final activity, we would like you to become a detective and find as many compound words as possible containing the word 'back'.

The word can be first or second. Grab a family member to join in and complete the activity together.

The more words you can create, the higher your rank.
See if you can make it to Superintendent!

0–5 Constable **6–10 Sergeant**

11–15 Inspector **16–20 Chief Inspector**

21+ Superintendent

Synonyms

What are synonyms?

A synonym means exactly or nearly the same as another word. For example, the words 'large', 'colossal' and 'massive' are synonyms of one another: they are synonymous. These words can be lifesavers, especially to stop you using the same word repetitively in a piece of writing. Synonym questions test your understanding of word meanings and word groups.

Worked example

In these questions, you need to choose **two** words that are closest in meaning. Choose one word from each group.

(weak, sturdy, minute)   (strong, frail, flexible)

The answer may be obvious but, once you've made a choice, try to put the words in the same sentence. In the example above, you could apply this sentence to double check the answer:

The carpenter made a **sturdy** wardrobe.

The carpenter made a **strong** wardrobe.

If the meaning remains the same, your choice is correct.

Challenge one: Synonym spider diagram

This activity will really get you considering how many synonyms you know. Find a friend or family member to challenge for this super synonym exercise.

Select the adjective or verb and see who can complete their synonym spider diagram first.

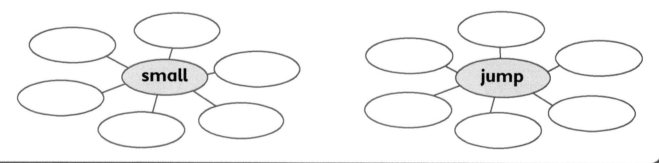

When we need a synonym for a word, we can use a thesaurus. Amazingly, in a typical thesaurus there are more than 145,000 entries – that is a lot of synonyms! Another fun fact is that the word 'thesaurus' comes from the Greek word for treasure and most definitely these wonderful books have a treasure trove of words!

Challenge two: Synonym swap

Exploring synonyms can be good fun and this challenge will help you consider an alternative synonym.

Read the sentences and try to replace as many of the underlined words as possible with a synonym. Remember, you shouldn't change the meaning.

a) The <u>spacious</u> room was <u>drafty</u> and <u>messy</u>.

_____

b) I <u>saw</u> ships and yachts <u>floating</u> on the <u>calm</u> sea.

_____

c) <u>Suddenly</u>, the <u>wooden</u> door opened with a <u>bang</u>.

_____

d) The <u>film</u> was really <u>frightening</u> and <u>exciting</u>.

_____

PUSH yourself: Select the synonym

This final activity will test your ability to select the best word to complete a sentence. Circle the most appropriate synonym for the sentence.

a) Manjeet (**pushed, played, forced**) his friend on the swing.

b) The tabby cat (**peeked, crept, crawled**) up on the minute mouse.

c) Clare (**smashed, banged, cracked**) the egg into the glass bowl.

d) Mum and I (**decorated, pierced, embellished**) the Christmas tree.

Tip

Using synonyms in your stories makes them more interesting. When answering 'closest in meaning questions', try to transfer one word at a time until you think you have a pair of synonyms.

Antonyms

What are antonyms?

Antonyms are words that have an opposite meaning (e.g. **happy** and **sad**). The term 'antonym' has its origin in an Ancient Greek word 'antonumia', which means 'counter name'.

Antonyms are used to express the opposite of a word and can be useful in your writing to make comparisons. Using words that are opposite can help to describe and explain in a way that creates a clearer image in the reader's mind.

Worked example

In this question, find **two** words, one from each group, that are most opposite in meaning.

(behind, near, before)   (close, after, underneath)

Be careful not to be drawn into spotting the synonym pair. In this example, you can see 'near' and 'close' would be closest in meaning. Check your answer and make sure the words are *opposites*. The answer is **before** and **after**.

Challenge one: Antonym pairs

To make you consider opposites, try to match one word in the first column to its opposite in the second column. The first one has been completed for you.

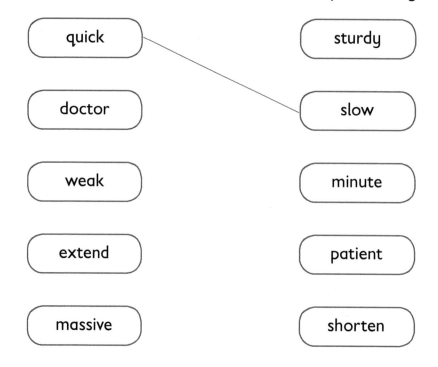

quick	sturdy
doctor	slow
weak	minute
extend	patient
massive	shorten

Did you know you can have different types of antonyms? One type is called 'graded' antonyms, and these are words that allow for shades of oppositeness. An example could be antonyms for the word 'good'.

unsatisfactory, poor, bad, terrible

Can you think of any other antonyms that could be graded? There are examples in the answers at the back of the book.

Challenge two: The power of prefixes

Prefixes are a group of letters that change the meaning of a word when they are added to the start.

Often if a prefix is added to a word, it can make it mean the opposite.

Can you add the correct prefix from the box to the words below? Use each prefix once only.

> dis   un   im   un

a) _____pleasure   **c)** _____able

b) _____polite   **d)** _____likely

PUSH yourself: Complementary antonyms

Another type of antonym is 'complementary' antonyms. These offer very little wriggle room and there is often only one antonym for each word. To really push yourself, can you record the complementary antonym next to the words below?

a) husband /_____

b) man /_____

c) dead /_____

d) predator /_____

e) off /_____

f) buy /_____

Can you think of any other complementary antonym pairs?

Tip

Learning antonyms is an excellent way to expand your vocabulary. Looking at the antonyms of a difficult word is a good way to confirm its meaning.

Odd Two Out

How do we solve odd two out questions?

Finding the odd two out is all about word classification. There will be five words and three will be associated or related in some way. This will leave two words that are the odd ones out (these words don't have to link together).

Worked example

Look at the five words below. Three of them are linked in some way.

Find the two words that do not go with these three.

start   halt   commence   terminus   begin

First, ask yourself what all the five words mean. See if you can group three words together through a common link. It is clear that three words mean the same: 'start', 'commence' and 'begin' are synonyms for go ahead. Therefore, this leaves **halt** and **terminus** as the two odd ones out.

Challenge one: Collecting categories

To test your grouping skills, arrange these words into five separate categories.

crimson	snooker	hawk	sow	kabaddi
squash	Essex	doe	osprey	Cornwall
cow	ruby	Yorkshire	red	falcon
Hampshire	eagle	scarlet	lacrosse	mare

1. _____ _____ _____ _____

2. _____ _____ _____ _____

3. _____ _____ _____ _____

4. _____ _____ _____ _____

5. _____ _____ _____ _____

Did you manage to group all the words correctly?

In these questions, it is important that you check if a word has more than one meaning, as this might determine how you group the words. One of the words in the English language with the most meanings is the verb 'set'. One particular dictionary had 430 definitions for it!

Challenge two: Word association

Some 11+ test questions may require you to find associations between words. A fun way to build a better awareness of links between words is to play a simple word association game with a friend or family member. The game can be played anywhere, in the car or at home as a time filler.

One player suggests a word like 'bicycle' and the next player has to come up with a linked word, such as 'tyre'. You could then add 'rubber' and your partner could then say 'eraser' to continue the chain.

This game can help you to think of alternative meanings of words, as demonstrated with 'rubber' as an 'eraser' rather than the material on a tyre.

PUSH yourself: Word themes

To help develop your general knowledge, this task can be done on your own or with somebody else. Select a category (some are listed below) and set yourself a time limit (e.g. 2 minutes) to write down as many words linked to the category as possible.

Girls' names

Boys' names

Countries in Europe

Countries in Asia

Countries in South America

Countries in Africa

Animals that live in a rainforest

Books written by a particular author

Famous landmarks around the world

Olympic sports

If you do this task with someone else, compare your list with theirs afterwards. Add their words to your list so that you can learn them.

Double Letter Series

Why is knowing the alphabet important for the 11+?

For some 11+ questions, you need to be able to count accurately and quickly (both forwards and backwards) through the letters of the alphabet. Being able to identify patterns and make deductions is also an important skill.

Worked example

The alphabet is given to help you with this question.

A B C D E F G H I J K L M N O P Q R S T U V W X Y Z

Try to work out the next pair of letters in the pattern.

PK   RL   TM   VN   (?)

To identify the pattern, start by looking at the first letters in each pair. See that these letters jump two forward and this can be recorded between the letters to clearly show the pattern (+2).

+2   +2   +2   +2

PK   RL   TM   VN   **X**

The next step is looking at the pattern from the second letter of each pair. In this sequence, we can see that these letters are consecutive (+1).

+1   +1   +1   +1

PK   RL   TM   VN   **XO**

Tip

Write the size of the jumps on the alphabet to help you see the pattern. Write above the alphabet for the first letters of each pair and below for the second letters of each pair.

Challenge one: Mirrored pairs

One variation in this question type is to spot when the letters in the alphabet are mirrored. If you split the alphabet between 'M' and 'N', it creates 13 pairs. Have a go at completing the table of mirrored letter pairs below.

A	B	C	D	E	F	G	H	I	J	K	L	M
				V			S				O	

An example of how this question type might look in an 11+ test is below.

A B C D E F G H I J K L M N O P Q R S T U V W X Y Z

EV is to **GT** as **IR** is to **?**

Challenge two: Counting on the alphabet

Counting accurately from one end of the alphabet to the other is a key skill for the 11+. If you have to count past the letter 'Z', you move to the letter 'A'. It is therefore easier to visualise the alphabet as a circle.

Here is a game to help you count along the alphabet correctly and can be fun to play with a friend or family member. All you need is a die, a piece of paper and some colouring pencils. First, write the alphabet out on a piece of paper. Each player rolls the die in turn and counts that number of letters along the alphabet starting from 'A'. The aim of the game is to reach the end of the alphabet first.

Player 1

A B C D E F G H I J K L M N O P Q R S T U V W X Y Z

Player 2

PUSH yourself: Alphabet game

This game will test your accuracy counting through the letters of the alphabet and is easy to play at home with another family member. Select the first page in a reading book and find the first two-letter word. Your partner needs to find the first two-letter word on page 2. Your score is found by counting how many letters in the alphabet separate the two letters in your word. The higher score wins. You can play round after round as you go through the pages of the book.

Multiple Meanings

How well do you know your words?

Knowing the different meanings of words with the same spelling is a key skill for the 11+ test. Here we will explore a question type that relies on this knowledge.

Worked example

There are two pairs of words in brackets. Only **one** of the five possible answers will go equally well with **both** pairs.

(sway   swing)   (stone   pebble)

stagger   rock   reel   lurch   robust

Read the words in the brackets and consider what these words mean and what is the same about them. Also think about the double meanings of words to help you see the links. Test each answer option against all the words in brackets. A useful way of doing this is to try each word in turn in the same sentence. If the sentences all make sense, then this is your answer.

The correct answer to this example is **rock**. Can you see why?

Tip

These questions can take a long time, so scan the answer options quickly and try to link them to the two pairs of words. Do this mentally because writing it down will waste valuable time.

Challenge one: Silly sentences!

Replace the underlined word in each sentence with the correct word from the box. The two words can have similar or different meanings, depending on the context.

brush	coat	trunk	box	mean	passage

a) The boys quickly dashed down the dark, narrow <u>chapter</u>.   _____

b) The teacher was very <u>average</u> setting all this English homework.   _____

c) The <u>jacket</u> of paint would take approximately two hours to dry.   _____

d) I purchased a hair <u>sweep</u>.   _____

e) The <u>suitcase</u> was the best place to saw the pine tree.   _____

f) The heavyweight fighter had been training to <u>container</u> for 10 years.   _____

Challenge two: Synonyms match

In this question type, you need to have a good understanding of synonyms.

Draw lines to match each word in the first column to its synonym in the second column. See if you can complete this task in 2 minutes.

chaos	injury
change	strike
benefit	end
contract	margin
hit	havoc
wound	gain
ample	shrink
emerge	plenty
conclusion	appear
edge	amend

PUSH yourself: Dual meaning

For words that have more than one meaning, knowing the less common definition(s) is the tricky part. See if you can record two different definitions for the words in the table.

address	
badger	
clip	
crane	
date	
engaged	
fall	
leaves	

Reshuffled Sentences

Can you make sense of a jumbled sentence?

In reshuffled sentences questions, you are given a sentence that has been jumbled up.
Often, you then need to reorder the words correctly and find the word that is not required.

Worked example

Look at the following sentence and identify the word which does not fit.

are   hour   rush   in   trains   the   packed   times

The correctly reordered sentence would be:
The trains are packed in rush hour.

So the word that is not required is **times**.

One strategy with these questions is to start by thinking about the subject of the sentence (but there might be more than one!). If that doesn't help, start by pairing verbs and adverbs, or adjectives and nouns. Sentences can start with a variety of different word groups; in this example it is an article.

Tip

Piecing together the sentence little by little can help to eliminate words and narrow down the answer options for you.

Tip

An article is a type of determiner. A determiner is a word that introduces a noun or provides information about the quantity of a noun (for example, 'an', 'few', 'many').

Challenge one: Word groups

Do you know the different word groups? In the following sentence, draw lines to join each word to its correct word group below.

(Daniel)   (won)   (the)   (annual)   (school)   (chess)   (tournament)

(verb) (adjective) (noun)   (noun)   (noun)   (noun)   (determiner)

There are eight word classes in the English language:

- nouns
- pronouns
- adjectives
- verbs
- adverbs
- prepositions
- conjunctions
- determiners.

Challenge two: Reorder the words

Reorder the words in these jumbled sentences. There are no extra words and you must use all the words given.

a) aren't crisps good sweets and you for

_____

b) late Scarlet her was lesson for clarinet

_____

c) people cereal like lots of breakfast for

_____

PUSH yourself: Unscramble the sentence

Unscramble the sentences. Circle the word that does not belong in each sentence.

a) beautiful garden Neera old lives cottage in an

b) Jonathan sisters or and brother one two has

c) group runs Tom's the owns mum local beaver

Tip

Often in these questions, two words are included to confuse you. For example, **tomorrow** and **yesterday**. Use your logic to work out the word that best fits.

Number Series

How nimble are you with numbers?

The Verbal Reasoning section of the 11+ test may include some number problems. Logical thinking, problem solving and identifying patterns are all skills needed in these questions. You will need to use good deduction and analytical skills to work out the rules and complete the number patterns.

Worked example

Find the number that continues the sequence in the most sensible way.

10, 19, 28, 37, 46, (?)

Finding the difference between numbers in the sequence will often reveal the pattern. In this example, the next number is 9 more than the previous number.

So the answer here is **55**.

Challenge one: Four operations

Insert the correct operation ($\div$, $\times$, $-$ or $+$) to make each statement correct.

a) 7 ☐ 6 = 42

b) 19 ☐ 6 = 13

c) (18 ☐ 3) ☐ 6 = 12

d) 56 ☐ 7 = 8

e) 24 ☐ 23 = 47

f) (34 ☐ 13) ☐ 7 = 3

Tip

Remember that you should complete any operations in brackets before doing the rest of the calculation.

Challenge two: Negative numbers

Number sequences can include negative numbers. Can you complete the gaps in the following sequence?

_____, −12, _____, −4, 0, 4, _____

Fibonacci numbers are named after an Italian mathematician called Leonardo of Pisa (better known as Fibonacci), who introduced them to western Europe after they had earlier been described by Indian mathematicians. They are related to the golden ratio and proceed in the following order: 0, 1, 1, 2, 3, 5, 8, 13, …

Can you see how the sequence works?

Challenge three: Special numbers

Sometimes finding the difference between numbers in a sequence doesn't reveal the pattern. Knowing special numbers will help you to spot more complex sequences.

Match the correct terms with the right sequence.

16, 25, 36, 49, 64, 81, 100, …

53, 59, 61, 67, 71, 73, …

27, 64, 125, 216, 343, …

0, 1, 1, 2, 3, 5, 8, 13, 21, 34, 55, …

cube numbers

prime numbers

Fibonacci

square numbers

PUSH yourself: Alternate sequence

Can you create some number sequences of your own? Try to explore different patterns and cover some of the variations shown in this topic.

Here is an example of an alternate sequence:

8, 3, 16, 6, 24, 9, 32, 12, 40, 15, 48, 18, (?)

Can you describe how the sequence works and find the next number?

_____

_____

_____

_____

_____

Tip

Practise your times tables to keep your number skills sharp. You can even practise when out in the car or on the bus, such as multiplying two of the numbers you see on a car number plate.

Insert the Letter

Can you find the missing letter?

In these types of 11+ questions, you have to add the same letter to two groups of letters to make four real words. Spelling knowledge and vocabulary are vital skills to answer these questions correctly.

Worked example

Insert the same letter into both pairs of brackets in order to complete the word in front of the brackets and begin the word after the brackets.

(sta [____] our)   (scar [____] ellow)

A good starting point is to look at the most unusual letter string you are given and then try different letters with it. For example, only a few letters could come before 'ellow'. These include **b**ellow, **f**ellow, **m**ellow and **y**ellow. By trying these different letters, you will find that only one forms four new words.

The answer is **y**.

Challenge one: Word snakes

Word snakes are a great way to create new words. They help you to make words that begin and end with the same letter. Here is a word snake using the letter 't':

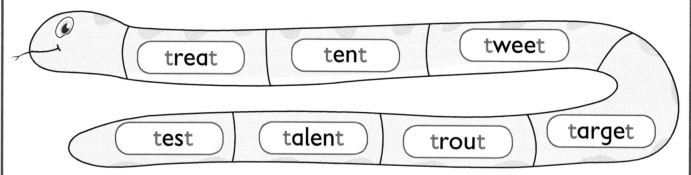

Can you make up your own word snake using the letter 'b'?

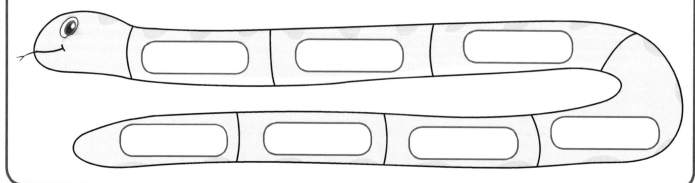

Challenge two: Letter strings

Letter strings are important in this question type.

Try to create a spider diagram of words that begin with the letter string **tr**.

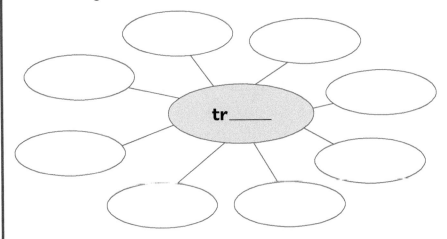

Now try to create a spider diagram of words that end with the letter string **lt**.

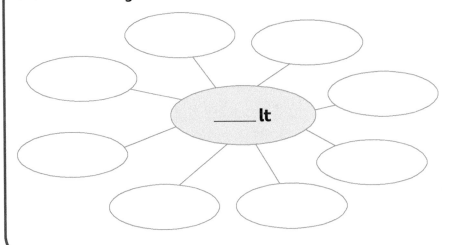

FUN FACT

Since there are lots more sounds than letters, many letters have different pronunciations. The **26** letters of the English alphabet make up more than **40** distinct sounds. For example, 'c' in **c**ool sounds different to the 'c' in **c**ity.

PUSH yourself: Missing letters

To really give you a harder challenge, try to solve these questions below.

Rather than inserting one letter, you have to place the same two letters in each pair of brackets on the same row.

a) (length [____] sure)   (fast [____] emy)

b) (coa ____] age)   (moi [____] eer)

c) (cel [____] cked)   (hel [____] af)

Tip

Remember, you don't always have to start with the first set of brackets. You can start with the second set and try to find these words first.

59

Thinking Logically

Are you a good fact-finder?

For logic questions, you need good deduction skills to work out the answers. You will be presented with some information and will have to work systematically by picking out only the relevant statements. Importantly, you must stick to the facts provided and not make any assumptions!

Worked example

Read the following information, then select the correct answer to the question.

At Heathfield School, Harry asked his five friends about their favourite fruit. Kane and Kris enjoy eating oranges and bananas. Only Kris likes apples. Poppy dislikes grapes but knows all fruit helps to protect you from illness. Sanjit likes what Poppy dislikes and devouring pears. Rupert and Poppy adore strawberries.

Who likes the most types of fruit?

A Kane   **B** Kris   **C** Poppy   **D** Sanjit   **E** Rupert

It can be useful before reading the information to find out what you are being asked to do. In this question, you must work out who likes the most types of fruit. One way to keep track of who likes what is to create a simple tally chart.

Ka	II
Kr	III
P	I
S	II
R	I

There are some statements that are not relevant. For example, '*but knows all fruit helps to protect you from illness*'. You can double check the tally chart against the question to make sure it is accurate. The answer is **B** as Kris likes oranges, bananas and apples.

Challenge one: Solve the riddle

Deciphering the information you are given is a key part of successfully solving these questions. Try the riddle below and use your logic to solve it!

When Thomas was 6 years old, his sister Leah was half his age.

If Thomas is 40 years old today, how old is Leah?

_____

Challenge two: Fact or fiction?

It is important to distinguish between fact and fiction in these questions. In the advert below, underline the facts in a red pen and the fictional parts in blue.

Buy the new Superclean bathroom cleaner! It'll leave your bathroom cleaner than any other! Superclean uses a mixture of soap and bleach that completely removes any sign of dust and grime. You won't be able to believe your eyes when you see what Superclean can do for you. Only £2.99 a bottle!

PUSH yourself: True statement

In these types of logic question, you are given some information to read and you need to work out which statement is true. These are very common in 11+ tests.

Three friends, Jasper, Julian and Jun, participate in numerous clubs at their school during the week. Each club only happens once in the five weekdays. Jasper attends chess on a Wednesday and one other club. Only Julian and Jun enjoy rugby and football respectively on consecutive days. Each day only has one club running. Jun swims on Tuesday but the others don't attend any club on this day.

Which of the following statements **must** be true?

A Jasper takes part in a club on Monday.

B Jasper only attends one club.

C Julian and Jun play rugby on Thursday.

D Julian and Jun play rugby on Friday.

E Jasper swims with Jun on a Tuesday.

Try this fun logic puzzle.

What is the number of the parking spot that the car is in?

| 161 | 061 | 681 | 881 | | 981 |

Introduction to Non-Verbal Reasoning

What is NVR?

'Non-Verbal Reasoning' or 'NVR' is the name for an 11+ topic where you are tested with questions full of images, shapes and patterns (rather than words or numbers).

Worked example

NVR tests how well you work with shapes and patterns.

Can you spot what has changed from Figure A to Figure B?

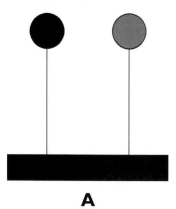

A

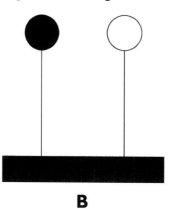

B

Although the general outline of the shape is identical, the red circle in Figure A has turned into a white circle in Figure B. So the two shapes are **connected** in that they have the same outline, but they are **different** in their shading.

Tip

Looking at ways in which shapes are connected is a good way of understanding what some of NVR is about. Work out what the figures have in common and how they are slightly different.

Challenge one: Patterns and sequences

Describe the sequence that is happening in these figures.

I

2

3

4

Which of these would be in Figure 4 to **continue the sequence**? Circle your answer.

A

B

C

Challenge two: Sides on a shape

Sometimes **the number of sides** on a shape is at the heart of an NVR question.

A

B

How many more sides does Figure B have than Figure A?

_____

Tip

Spotting sequences can seem tricky at first, but in fact there are a few common themes to look out for – and we will be covering them all in the following pages!

Tip

The number of sides on a shape is an important thing to look out for in NVR questions. This could be a key part of a sequence or transformation.

PUSH yourself: What is happening in the sequence?

The figures below are in a sequence. Two things are happening in the sequence. Can you spot what they are?

1   2   3   4

_____

_____

Odd One Out

Can you find the one that doesn't fit?

Odd one out is a type of question where you are given a set of figures and all but one of them have something in common. You need to work out the 'odd one out' – the figure that does not share the common feature(s).

Worked example

Which one of these figures is the odd one out?

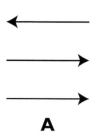

A

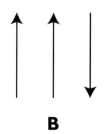

B

C

The answer is **C** because it contains a different type of arrow than the other two figures.

Challenge one: Spot the difference

Can you spot the difference between these two figures?

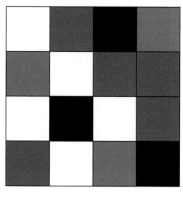

A

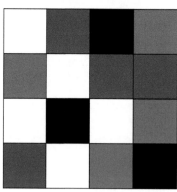

B

At first glance the figures look identical, but if you examine them closely, you will see that there is a difference. The correct answer is at the back of the book.

Tip

Go through the figures and **rule things out**. Considering the worked example above, are all the arrows pointing in the same direction in two of the figures and not in the other? No. Are the arrows of the same colour in two of the figures and a different one in the third? No. By going through these, you will spot what is the same in two figures and different in the other – in this case, the type of arrow.

Challenge two: Create your own 'odd one out' puzzle

Find a long piece of string and cut it into three equal-sized sections (ask an adult to help you stay safe with the scissors).

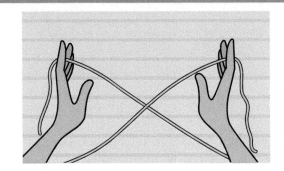

Imagine you are creating an 'odd one out' question yourself. What can you do to two pieces of the string that you do not do to the third?

You could try these variations:

- paint two a different colour
- cut one shorter than the other two
- lay all three pieces of string flat on a table and give two of them the same number of loops or crossovers.

You might create a question like this:

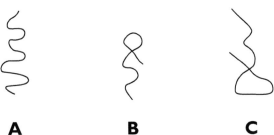

| A | B | C |

Which is the odd one out here? Circle your answer.

PUSH yourself: Find the odd one out

Try to solve this trickier question.

Four of the figures are identical and one is not. Which figure is the odd one out? Circle your answer.

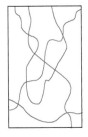 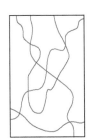 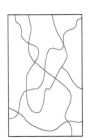 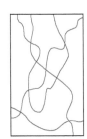 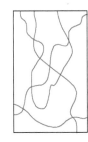

| A | B | C | D | E |

Series

What are series?

In **series** questions, you are presented with a row of figures that follow a sequence. One of the figures will be blank (usually with a question mark) and you need to work out which of the answer options should go into that blank to continue the sequence.

Worked example

Which figure should replace the question mark to correctly complete the series?

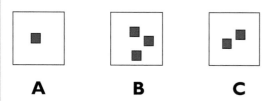

A   **B**   **C**

There is one fewer square as you move along the series from left to right. Therefore the answer is **A**.

Tip

Like most of NVR, when you are trying to work out the sequence in the series, there are certain themes to consider. Could it be the number of shapes, the number of sides, patterns of shading, the number of intersections, or the same shape rotating? Work through them one at a time to rule them out until you find the right one.

Challenge one: Spot the sequence

Can you work out the sequence in these figures?

Clue: This is a **position** sequence.

The correct answer can be found at the back of the book.

Challenge two: Create your own series!

Find (or borrow) some building blocks and create your own series with them. Create four different arrangements of blocks so that they each create a sequence. Do one for each of these themes:

- a sequence where more blocks are added each time
- a sequence where there are fewer blocks each time
- a sequence involving the position of blocks
- a sequence where more or fewer blocks are touching each time.

You may have created a question like this:

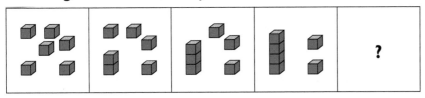

Which figure replaces the blank in the series above? Circle your answer.

A

B

C

PUSH yourself: Missing figure in the middle

Now see if you can solve this trickier series question.

Which figure completes the series? Circle your answer.

  ?

A

B

C

The correct answer is at the back of the book.

Tip

When the missing figure is in the middle of the series, try to spot a possible sequence from the first figure to the second. Then see if that same sequence works from the fourth to the fifth figure.

Rotations

Can you get your head around rotations?

In **rotations** questions, you have to work out which answer option is a rotation of the figure that you are given. Sounds easy? Surprisingly, it can be quite tricky – but the following sections will help you to solve them.

Worked example

A rotation involves turning an object around a central point. For example, if you place a pencil on a table, and turn it so that the nib now points 90 degrees to the right, you are rotating it by 90 degrees clockwise.

Which of these shapes is a rotation of the shape on the left?

A   **B**   **C**

Hang on – aren't they all a rotation of the rabbit? In fact, look again. They aren't! Only Figure **A** is a rotation of the rabbit – the rest are not. Turn the book around so you can see why – or concentrate on the ears!

Challenge one: Have a turn!

Which figure (A, B or C) is a rotation of the first figure you are given? Circle your answer.

A   **B**   **C**

Clue: Work out which answer options are not rotations. Concentrate on the short stem of the tick shape – which options do not fit on the rotation of the given shape?

The correct answer is at the back of the book.

Tip

A 'red herring' is an answer option that is close to being correct and is deliberately given to try to trick you, so watch out for these. In the worked example, answer options B and C are the red herrings. With most rotation questions, a red herring will involve the same shape, but it may have been **inverted** (flipped over) and **then rotated** – so it cannot be the right answer.

Challenge two: Turn your hand to a rotation

Draw an interesting shape on a piece of paper (make it quite large). Make sure the shape has a stem with a line coming off it – it makes it easier to understand the rotation issue. Then cut out the shape. Now rotate it in 90-degree turns.
Then **flip the shape over** and rotate the shape in 90-degree turns. Pay particular attention to your stem with a line. Can you see the difference?

You could create a question like this:

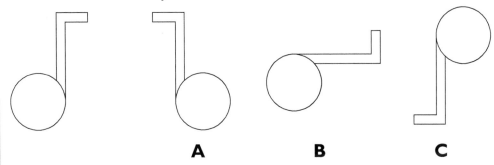

A   **B**   **C**

Which of these figures is a rotation of the figure on the left? Circle your answer.

PUSH yourself: Trickier rotation

Now see if you can solve this trickier rotation question! Which figure (A, B, C, D or E) is a rotation of the first figure you are given? Circle your answer.

A   **B**   **C**   **D**   **E**

Clue: Look closely at the red smaller shape and where it sits on the original figure. Once more, the red herrings are rotations of the original shape when it has been flipped over.

The correct answer is at the back of the book.

Tip

Understanding **clockwise** and **anticlockwise** rotations will help you in many NVR questions. Just look at the direction of a clock's hand movements and you will quickly grasp which way clockwise means.

Reflections

Can you reflect?

In **reflections** questions, you have to work out which figure in the answer options is a reflection of the shape presented through the mirror line. These need a lot of practice!

Imagine placing a real-life mirror on the mirror line. What would the object look like?

Worked example

Which figure is a reflection of the shape on the left through the given mirror line?

| | A | B | C |

If you put a mirror where the line is, you would see Figure C as a reflection of the shape. Therefore, the answer is **C**.

Challenge one: Time to reflect!

Which figure is a reflection of the shape on the left? Circle your answer.

A   B   C

Tip

Reflections can get quite complicated. Make things easier by just concentrating on certain aspects of the main shape – perhaps a curve or a diagonal line. If this is not reflected properly in a certain answer figure, you can rule that option out.

Challenge two: Make your own reflection!

Draw a large shape with some interesting features (perhaps stems, again) and then cut it out. Now manipulate it so you would see what it looked like as a reflection. If you have a small mirror to hand, even better!

Imagine you were setting a question to trick a friend. What other answer options would you create to try to fool them?

You may have created a question like this:

A **B** **C**

Which figure is a reflection of the shape on the left? Circle your answer.

PUSH yourself: Trickier reflection

Now see if you can solve this trickier question!

Which figure is a reflection of the shape on the left? Circle your answer.

A **B** **C** **D** **E**

Clue: First rule out some of the figures. Concentrate on the foot shape first – which ones are not reflections of the foot? Then look at the triangles and rule out other options until you get the right answer.

The correct answer is at the back of the book.

Matrices

What are matrices?

In **matrices** questions, you are presented with a grid (made up of 2 × 2 or 3 × 3 squares) with figures in all but one square. The figures will follow a pattern of some sort. You need to work out the pattern and find the missing figure in the grid.

Worked example

Which of the figures on the right should go into the empty square?

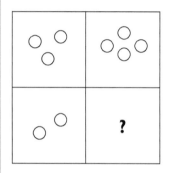

A   **B**   **C**

You need to solve the pattern. If you move down the left column from top to bottom, you can see that there is one fewer circle. So the correct answer is **B**, as it has one fewer circle than the figure at the top of the right column.

Challenge one: What goes in the grid?

Which figure should go in the missing square in the grid? Circle your answer.

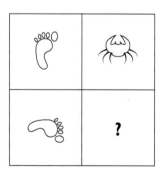

A   **B**   **C**

Tip

With matrices questions, you need to check for patterns that go from top to bottom in the columns, or from left to right in the rows. This is also true for 3 × 3 grid matrices.

Tip

Using your skills from other NVR topics will help you solve matrices questions. In particular, remember your rotation, reflection and sequence skills.

Challenge two: Make a matrix!

Grab some pencils, paper and a ruler and create your own 2 × 2 grid. Then build a question all of your own. Try to use a theme already covered in this book, for example:

- series
- rotation
- reflection

You may have created a question like this:

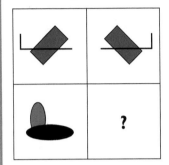

A

B

C

Which figure completes the grid? Circle your answer.

PUSH yourself: Trickier matrix

Now try this trickier question!

Which figure completes the grid? Circle your answer.

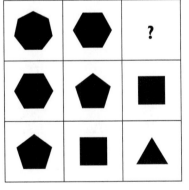

A

B

C

D

E

Clue: Work down from the top to the bottom of the columns.

The correct answer can be found at the back of the book.

Analogies

What are analogies?

In **analogies** questions, you are presented with a figure that is then changed in some way to make a second figure. You need to work out what it is that has changed. Then you are presented with a third shape and you need to change that shape in the same way. An analogy offers you the connection – for example, car is to road as train is to track. As the analogy with car is road, we know it must be track for train, as that is what each type of vehicle travels on.

Tip

Look out for common NVR themes in the change(s) to the original shape. For example, it could be position, shading, reflection, rotation, or intersection.

Worked example

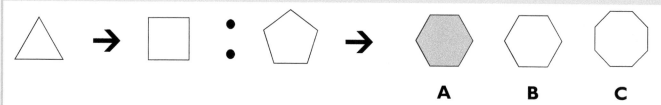

You can see that the triangle has changed to a square, so it has increased by one side. So we take the 'test shape' after the colon and add one side to it. The original shape did not change colour so the answer must be **B**.

Challenge one: Analogies with string

The first figure on the left has been changed in some way to create the second figure. Make the same change to the third figure to find the correct answer.
Circle your answer.

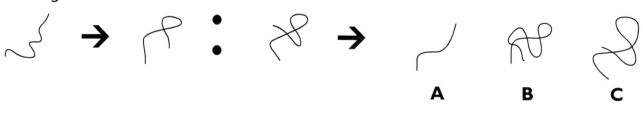

Challenge two: Using change to make some changes!

Get hold of as much loose change as you can – preferably in different denominations of coins, such as 1p, 2p, 5p, 10p, 20p, and so on.

Make one pile full of a different amount and type of coins.

Make a second pile with a different amount and type of coins.

What is the difference between the first pile and the second pile? It could be:

- a difference in the total value
- a difference in the number of a certain type of coin
- a difference in the size of the coin pile.

Then make a third pile of a different amount and type of coins. For your fourth pile, make the same changes as for your first and second piles. That is your analogy!

If it was a difference in the size of the coin pile, it could translate to something like this:

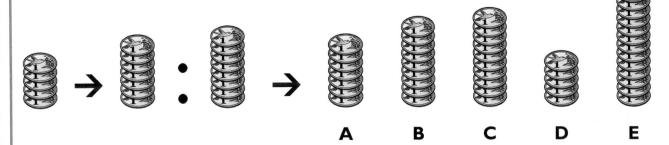

Which is the answer to this analogies puzzle? The correct answer is at the back of the book.

PUSH yourself: Trickier analogy

Now try this trickier question!

The first figure on the left has been changed in some way to create the second figure. Make the same change to the third figure to find the correct answer. Circle your answer.

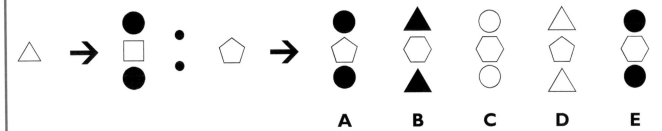

Clue: There are two things going on here – one to the outlined shape and one above and below it.

The correct answer is at the back of the book.

Codes

Can you crack the codes?

In **codes** questions, you have to be like a spy and crack the secret code! You will be presented with figures that are coded by letters. You have to work out what feature each letter represents. It could be the position of a shape, the number of shapes, the number of sides, the shading, and so on. Then you have to work out the code for the new shape you are presented with.

Worked example

Look at these codes for the figures in the boxes. Can you work out what the codes A, B, C and D stand for?

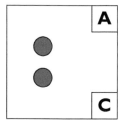 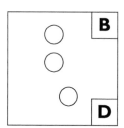 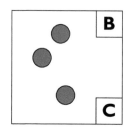

A is the code for two circles and B is the code for three circles.

C is the code for red circles and D is the code for white circles.

Tip

Look for where there are two instances of the code. So in the top row of this example, there are two B codes. Now work out what is the same in those two figures, as that must be what B represents.

Challenge one: Code finding

Look at the codes for the three figures on the left. Which code on the right should go in the empty boxes of the fourth figure?

   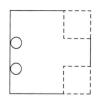

                                                  A   B   C

Clue: Look out for the number and position of the circles.

The correct answer is at the back of the book.

Challenge two: Create your own codes!

You can create your own codes question with everyday objects. First, grab some paper and write down your code letters. Then find some objects, for example pens and pencils. Put two pens in one pile, another pen in a second pile and two pencils in a third pile.

Now put your codes alongside them:

- a code for pens
- a code for pencils
- a code for two objects
- a code for one object.

You will see that you have created your own 'red herring' – colours are not part of the codes. It won't matter what colour your pens and pencils are! Now make a fourth pile and ask someone to crack your code – what should the codes be for your fourth pile?

You may have created something like this:

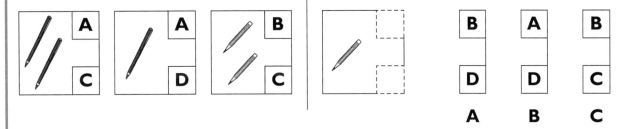

Look at the codes for the three figures on the left and work out the correct code for the fourth figure. Circle your answer.

PUSH yourself: Trickier codes

Now have a go at this trickier question!

Look at the codes for the four figures on the left and work out the correct code for the fifth figure. Circle your answer.

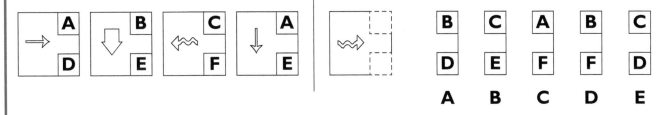

Clue: Look at the type of arrows and the direction they are pointing in!

The correct answer is at the back of the book.

Hidden Shapes

Can you spot the shape?

In **hidden shapes** questions, a certain shape is hidden within one of the figures in the answer options. You have to find the figure that contains the shape. The shape will not be reflected but it could be rotated.

Worked example

Which figure is hiding this shape?

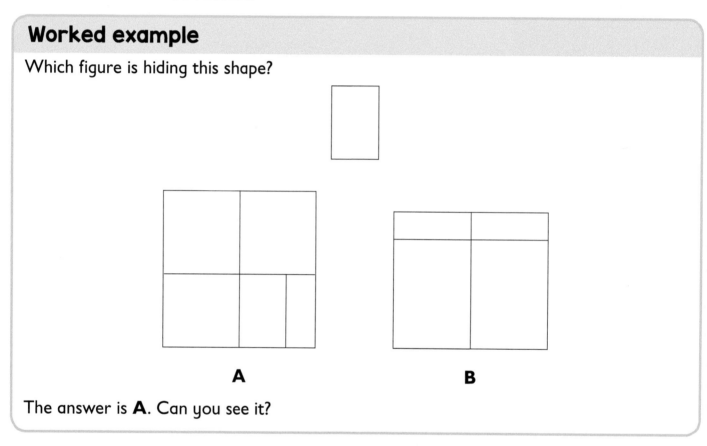

A   B

The answer is **A**. Can you see it?

Challenge one: Hide and seek!

Which figure is hiding the given shape? Circle your answer.

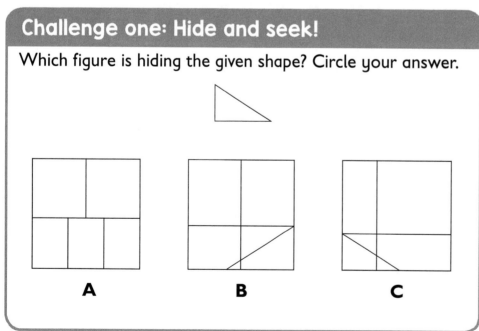

A   B   C

Tip

Look for certain distinctive elements of the shape you are trying to find – perhaps the angle of a diagonal line, or a curve – and then look for that shape in any of the answer options. It will help you to rule out some places to examine!

Challenge two: Hide your own shape!

Using pencils, paper and a ruler, try drawing your own combinations of shapes and lines in three different squares. Then 'hide' your own shape within one of them. Test it out on your family and see if they can spot where it is! Remember to accurately draw the shape you have hidden, so they know what to look for.

You may have drawn something like this:

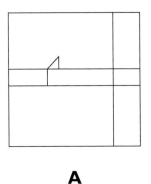

A

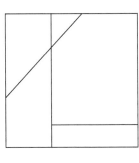

B

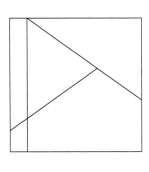

C

In which figure is this shape hidden?

Circle your answer.

PUSH yourself: Trickier hidden shape

Now try this trickier question!

Find the figure in which the given shape is hidden. Circle your answer.

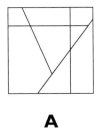

A

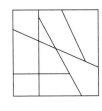

B

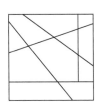

C

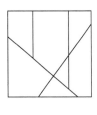

D

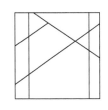

E

Clue: Look for the diagonal sides of the hidden shape because they are likely to be easier to spot than the straight horizontal and vertical sides.

The correct answer is at the back of the book.

Mixed Activities

1. **Read this passage carefully and answer the questions that follow.**

   An extract from *Alice's Adventures in Wonderland* by Lewis Carroll

   There was a table set out under a tree in front of the house, and the March Hare and the Hatter were having tea at it: a Dormouse was sitting between them, fast asleep, and the other two were using it as a cushion, resting their elbows on it, and talking over its head. "Very uncomfortable for the Dormouse," thought Alice; "only, as it's asleep, I suppose it doesn't mind."

   The table was a large one, but the three were all crowded together at one corner of it: "No room! No room!" they cried out when they saw Alice coming. "There's *plenty* of room!" said Alice indignantly, and she sat down in a large armchair at one end of the table.

   Circle the letter that matches the correct answer.

   a) Where was the tea party taking place?

   A In front of a tree   **C** In front of the house

   B Behind the house   **D** Next to a tree

   b) Why did Alice think the Dormouse might be uncomfortable?

   A It was asleep at the table

   B It was in a stiff armchair

   C The March Hare and the Hatter were resting their elbows on it

   D They were all crowded together at one corner of the table

   c) Both the table and the armchair are described as 'large'. Which word below is a synonym for 'large'?

   A miniscule   **C** petite

   B meagre   **D** great

2. **Work out the next numbers in these sequences.**

   a) 64, 81, 100, 121, 144, (?)   _____

   b) 17, 19, 23, 29, 31, 37, 41, (?)   _____

   c) 7, 8, 14, 16, 21, 24, 28, (?)   _____

   d) 6, 7, 13, 20, 33, 53, (?)   _____

3. In each part, underline two words that go together to form a new word. Underline one word from the first set of brackets and one word from the second set of brackets.

   a) (hope, prove, keep)   (less, full, out)

   b) (owl, watch, clock)   (time, wise, look)

   c) (white, black, up)   (down, coal, bird)

4. Which one of these figures Is the odd one out? Circle your answer.

 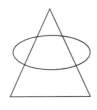 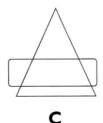  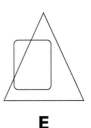

   A   **B**   **C**   **D**   **E**

5. Read the passage and choose the correct option that fills each of the gaps.

   An extract from *The Jungle Book* by Rudyard Kipling

   There was a chorus of deep growls, and a young wolf in his fourth year flung back Shere Khan's ____a)____ to Akela: "What have the Free People to do with a man's cub?" Now, the Law of the Jungle lays down that if there is any dispute as to the right of a cub to be accepted by the Pack, he must be spoken for by at least two members of the Pack who are not his ____b)____ and mother.

   "Who speaks for this cub?" said Akela. "Among the Free People who speaks?" There was no answer and Mother Wolf got ready for what she knew would be her last ____c)____, if things came to fighting.

   a) statement   answer   question

   b) father   brother   kin

   c) roar   fight   kiss

6. Record the exact time of this analogue clock. Write the time in both words and figures.

Words: _____

Figures: _____

7. In each part, choose the *two* words that are most similar in meaning. You should underline one word from the first set of brackets and one word from the second set of brackets.

a) (reject, accept, card)   (issue, decline, reverse)

b) (dissolve, deliberate, depreciate)   (thoughtless, weak, purposeful)

c) (remove, evaluate, evaluation)   (assessment, neglect, ignore)

8. Which figure on the right should go in the blank square on the left to complete the series? Circle your answer.

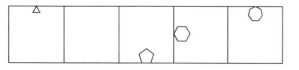

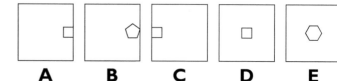

A   B   C   D   E

9. **Read the passage and fill in each of the gaps using words from the word bank.**

saddle	skip	still	hat	trot
not	slow	teenager	woman	bent

An extract from *Black Beauty* by Anna Sewell

Every one may not know what breaking in is, therefore I will describe it. It means to teach a horse to wear a **a)**_____ and bridle, and to carry on his back a man, **b)**_____ or child; to go just the way they wish, and to go quietly. Besides this, he has to learn to wear a collar, a crupper, and a breeching, and to stand **c)**_____ while they are put on; then to have a cart or a chaise fixed behind, so that he cannot walk or **d)**_____ without dragging it after him; and he must go fast or **e)**_____, just as his driver wishes.

10. **Draw a shape in which the area is numerically equal to its perimeter.**

11. **In each part, choose the *two* words that are most opposite in meaning. You should underline one word from the first set of brackets and one word from the second set of brackets.**

a) (people, plural, position)   (singular, location, mankind)

b) (continue, seek, signpost)   (proceed, postpone, postmark)

c) (ignited, aggressive, ignorant)   (uneducated, educated, impolite)

12. **Which of the figures on the right is a rotation of the figure on the left?**
    Circle your answer.

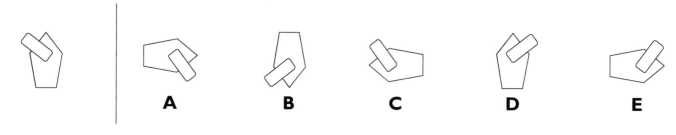

A   B   C   D   E

13. **Fill in the missing letters to complete the passage below.**

An extract from *The Railway Children* by E. Nesbit

It was one day when Mother had gone to Maidbridge. She had gone alone, but the children were to go to the station to meet her. And, loving the **a)** s_ _ _ ion as they did, it was only natural that they should be there a good hour before there was any chance of Mother's **b)** tr_ _n arriving, even if the train were punctual, which was most unlikely. No doubt they would have been just as early, even if it had been a fine day, and all the delights of woods and fields and rocks and rivers had been open to them. But it happened to be a very wet day and, for July, very cold. There was a wild **c)** w_ _d that drove flocks of dark purple **d)** c_ _ _d s across the sky "like herds of dream-elephants," as Phyllis said. And the rain stung sharply, so that the way to the station was finished at a run.

14. **What is the name of this shape?**

_____

15. **In each part, three of the five words are linked in some way. Find and underline the two words that do not go with these three.**

a) vixen   mare   hen   cygnet   foal

b) massive   compact   vast   microscopic   large

c) quill   pen   eraser   pencil   sharpener

16. **Which of the figures on the right is a reflection of the figure on the left? Circle your answer.**

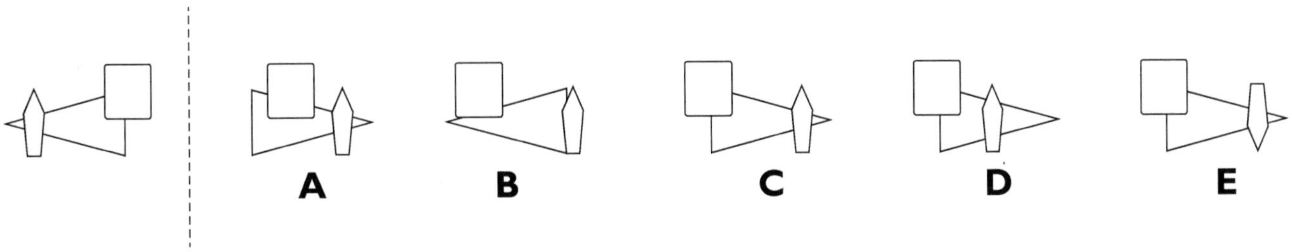

A   B   C   D   E

17. **Can you fill in each of the spaces in this poem so that the missing word rhymes with the word at the end of the line above?**

An extract from 'The Night Before Christmas' by Clement Clarke Moore

'Twas the night before Christmas, and all through the house,

Not a creature was stirring, not even a _____.

The stockings were hung by the chimney with care,

In the hope that St. Nicholas soon would be _____.

The children were nestled all snug in their beds,

While visions of sugar-plums danced in their _____.

And mamma in her 'kerchief, and I in my cap,

Had just settled our brains for a long winter's _____;

18. **Solve the following questions.**

a) Find 1% of 200   _____

b) What is 25% of 800?   _____

c) Find half (50%) of £144 _____

d) Calculate 40% of 70 km   _____

e) Find 20% of 1,000 m   _____

19. **The alphabet has been provided to support you with this question.**

A B C D E F G H I J K L M N O P Q R S T U V W X Y Z

Work out the next letter pair in each pattern.

a) ZM   AN   BP   CS   (?)   _____

b) SA   RZ   PY   MX   (?)   _____

c) UF   SH   QJ   OL   (?)   _____

20. **Which of the figures on the right fills the blank space in the grid on the left? Circle your answer.**

21. **Read the following sentence and answer the questions below.**

   The large black dog raced along the winding path.

   a) Find the **three** adjectives in this sentence. _____ _____ _____

   b) Find the **two** nouns in this sentence. _____ _____

   c) Can you find the verb in this sentence? _____

22. **Use the given compass points to help you answer the questions below.**

   a) How many degrees are between North and South-East if travelling in a clockwise direction? _____

   b) Sophia is facing South-West and then turns clockwise 135°.

   Which compass direction is she now facing? _____

   c) Alessandro is walking in a north-westerly direction and he turns 180°.

   Which way is he now facing? _____

23. **In each part, there are two pairs of words in brackets. Only *one* of the five possible answers will go equally well with *both* pairs of words in brackets. Circle the correct answer.**

   a) (letter, message)   (tone, ring)

       colour   memo   note   mood   book

   b) (holiday, break)   (fall, topple)

       fly   swing   vacation   trip   descend

   c) (jacket, tunic)   (cover, paint)

       coat   varnish   blanket   smear   glaze

86

24. Work out how the first figure on the left changes to make the second figure. Then make the same change to the third figure. Circle the correct answer on the right.

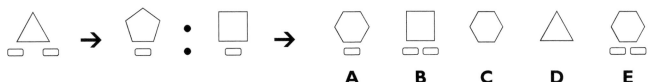

A   B   C   D   E

25. Find the five words that are spelt wrongly in the passage below. Write the correct spellings in the answer spaces. Look out for homophones!

> **An extract from *Jack and the Beanstalk* by Joseph Jacobs**
>
> Jack ran as fast as he could, and the ogre came rushing after, and wood soon have caught him; only Jack had a start and dodged him a bit and new where he was going. When he got to the beanstalk, the ogre was not more than twenty yards away when suddenly he sore Jack disappear like, and when he got up to the end of the rode he saw Jack underneath climing down for dear life.

_____ _____ _____ _____ _____

26. Look at the bar chart and answer the questions.

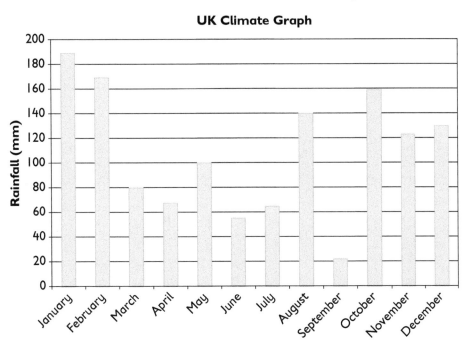

a) In which month did the highest amount of rainfall occur? _____

b) Which month had exactly 80 mm of rainfall? _____

c) How much more rainfall fell in October compared with May? _____

27. Look at each jumbled sentence and find the word which does not fit.

a) a Manraj's lot yesterday work takes him overseas _____

b) tallest class was Georgina hopes in her the _____

c) breakfast toast on favourite my bowl is jam _____

28. The four figures on the left each have a code. Work out the codes and find the correct code for the fifth figure. Circle your answer.

                                                    A   B   C   D   E

29. Each sentence below demonstrates a literary device. Circle which literary device is shown in each part.

a) The paper aeroplane soared like an eagle across the classroom.

   A metaphor   **B** simile   **C** personification   **D** onomatopoeia

b) The pig squealed as the farmer moved it.

   A metaphor   **B** simile   **C** personification   **D** onomatopoeia

c) The stars in the midnight sky winked at me cheekily.

   A metaphor   **B** simile   **C** personification   **D** onomatopoeia

d) The moon was a torch guiding me home.

   A metaphor   **B** simile   **C** personification   **D** onomatopoeia

30. The weights of eight children are shown in the table below.

Name	Amir	Lily	Pat	Fred	Kian	Beau	Raj	Anna
Weight (kg)	20	25	18	22	19	21	15	20

Work out the average weight of the children in kilograms. _____

31. Find the number that continues each sequence in the most sensible way.

a)   2, 5, 4, 10, 6, 15, 8, 20, (?)   _____

b)   89, 82, 75, 68, 61, 54, (?)   _____

c)   101, 102, 104, 107, 111, 116, (?)   _____

32. Look at the given shape. In which figure is this shape hidden? Circle your answer.

    A   **B**   **C**   **D**   **E**

33. In each part, insert the same letter into both sets of brackets. The letter should complete the word in front of the square brackets and begin the word after the square brackets. Write the letter in the space provided.

a) (dov [___] ra)   (for [___] arth)

b) (dra [___] heel)   (cla [___] aste)

c) (goa [___] one)   (bow [___] ack)

34. Answer these fractions questions.

a) $\frac{2}{3}$ of 24 = ?   _____

b) What is $\frac{2}{3}$ plus $\frac{3}{5}$ _____

c) Which is the smallest fraction in this list?

$\frac{1}{4}, \frac{1}{3}, \frac{5}{12}, \frac{4}{24}$ _____

35. Anika always leaves home before 8:15 am in the morning. She walks to a bus stop that is 10 minutes away. The bus journey to school is 20 minutes long. Hannah, who is in Anika's class, arrives by another form of transport and is never late. School starts at 8:50 am.

Which statement below **must** be true? Circle the letter for your answer.

A Hannah arrives at school at 8:55 am.

B Hannah and Anika both travel by bus.

C Anika can get to school by 8:50 am.

D Anika leaves for school at 8:20 am.

E Hannah's journey to school is 20 minutes long.

Answers

Pages 6–7: Comprehension

Challenge one

a) Answers may link to Cinderella.
b) Answers may involve the boy not doing as he is told and befriending a dragon.
c) Answers may involve the bird realising it has other great qualities besides flying.

Challenge two

A mouse disturbs a sleeping lion and begs for his life.	1
The lion then gets caught in a hunter's net.	4
The mouse hears the lion's roar.	6
The mouse chews the net.	7
The lion laughs disbelievingly but releases the mouse.	3
The mouse swears he will repay the kindness if the lion lets him go.	2
The lion is stuck and roars in anger.	5
The lion falls to the ground.	8

Push yourself

Answers will vary.

Pages 8–9: Fiction and Non-fiction

Challenge one

Fiction	Non-fiction
A play	A biography
A poem	A newspaper
A story	A reference book

Challenge two

Answers will vary. Examples:

a) Once the leaves die, they fall and begin to decay on the ground.
   Some birds migrate to warmer parts of the world before the winter arrives.
b) The setting sun slowly began to disappear behind the peaceful, rolling hills.
   The branches of the trees waved at a flock of birds flying overhead.

Push yourself

Answers will vary.

Pages 10–11: Poetry

Challenge one

Poems will vary.

Challenge two

Likely answers are: black; feet; trees; flies

Push yourself

Answers will vary.

Pages 12–13: Spelling

Challenge one

reached; packed; trains; different; People; fields; workers; by; soldiers; finally

Challenge two

Options joined as follows:
course – a route or direction followed
coarse – rough or harsh in texture
whole – all of something
hole – an opening or hollow place
heard – when you have made out sounds with your ear
herd – a large group of animals
stationary – not moving
stationery – writing and other office materials
guessed – to have estimated or concluded without all of the information
guest – someone who is invited to visit or stay

Push yourself

Answers will vary. Examples:
a) Rhythm Helps Your Two Hips Move
b) Never Eat Chips, Eat Salad Sandwiches And Raspberry Yogurt
c) Sleep, Eat, Play And Read And Take Exercise
d) Can A Lion Eat Nuts Daily And Roar?

Pages 14–15: Punctuation

Challenge one

Options joined as follows:
, – comma
: – colon
. – full stop
; – semi-colon
! – exclamation mark
? – question mark
( ) – brackets or parenthesis
" " – speech marks or inverted commas
… – ellipsis

Challenge two

It was dark outside; **or** : the sun had set hours ago. Ben's eyesight wasn't great, even with his glasses on. He needed to focus or he would not find his way out of the maze. What could possibly go wrong? "Stop right there!" a loud voice called.

Challenge three

a) My brother's dog is called Rover.
b) Did you sell Sarah's cake at the fair?
c) "I love the zoo," said Jessica excitedly.

Push yourself

Answers will vary.

Pages 16–17: Grammar

Challenge one

a) Yesterday, I bought my lunch at the shop.
b) Yesterday, I wrote in my diary.
c) Yesterday, I drank my juice.
d) Yesterday, I swam lengths in the pool.
e) Yesterday, I taught my friend to play chess.

Challenge two

a) Nouns: cat, boy
   Verbs: purred, stroked
   Adjectives: sleepy, young
   Adverb: loudly
b) Noun: feet, boy
   Verbs: rose, rubbed
   Adjective: attentive
   Adverb: lazily
c) Nouns: cat, time, dinner
   Verbs: stalked, see, was
   Adjective: black
   Adverb: slowly

Push yourself

Answers will vary.

Fun fact

Answers will vary. Example:
Brown jars prevented the mixture from freezing too quickly.

Pages 18–19: Word Groups

Challenge one

Nouns	Verbs	Adjectives	Adverbs
umbrella	sweeping	frozen	deliberately
octopus	sprinting	malicious	sometimes
bookcase	hurrying	fair	crossly

Challenge two

Answers will vary. Examples:

Word type	Example words
Articles	the, a, an
Nouns	chair, school, ball
Pronouns	he, she, they
Adjectives	spotty, huge, quiet
Verbs	chased, wrote, think
Adverbs	perfectly, softly, quickly
Conjunctions	and, because, but
Prepositions	under, on, in

Push yourself

Answers will vary.

Pages 20–21: Literary Devices

Challenge one

Answers may vary slightly from those shown below.

	woof
	ding dong
	splash
	sip / slurp
	knock knock
	peck

Challenge two

a) i)   The <u>street lights</u> glared at me wickedly in the dark night.
    ii) <u>Snowflakes</u> danced around me like little white ballerinas.
    iii) The <u>tree</u> reached its gnarled fingers toward me.
    iv) The <u>daffodils</u> swayed melodically in the spring breeze.
b) Own examples of personification will vary but could include:
   Tourists flocked to the beach as the sun smiled down on them.
   The alarm clock screamed in my ear as I struggled to wake up.
   Thunder roared through the sky as the storm passed over us.
   The leaves refused to stop falling as autumn began.
   The moon's twinkling light stretched across the hillside.

Push yourself

Answers will vary. Examples:
Two talented tortoises tried to tip-toe
Three thrushes threw a thrilling party
Four friendly frogs found it funny
Five flamingos fiddled with their feathers
Six slimy snakes slithered from under a stone
Seven swans sang a silly song
Eight aardvarks ate all they could
Nine newts showed their knobbly knees
Ten tigers turned up with treats of tea and toast!

Pages 22–23: Cloze

Challenge one

A soon **B** garden **C** delightful **D** end

Challenge two

beautiful; forest; window; hair; climbed

Push yourself

Answers will vary.

Pages 24–25: Understanding Number

Challenge one

1	8	3
5	12	7
6	4	2

Fun fact

quadrillion, quintillion, sextillion, septillion, octillion, nonillion, decillion and undecillion

Challenge two

Push Yourself

Balloon 51

Pages 26–27: Time

Challenge one

Lines drawn to join times as follows:

17:00 – 5 pm	21:00 – 9 pm
19:00 – 7 pm	13:00 – 1 pm
23:00 – 11 pm	03:00 – 3 am
08:00 – 8 am	14:00 – 2 pm

Challenge two

a) 21 minutes **b)** 15 minutes **c)** Train 2

Push yourself

a) 72 hours **c)** 600 seconds **e)** 120 minutes
b) 7 **d)** 10 years

Pages 28–29: Area and Perimeter

Fun fact

False

Challenge one

a) Perimeter: 14 cm — Area: 10 cm²
b) Perimeter: 8 cm — Area: 3 cm²
c) Perimeter: 8 cm — Area: 4 cm²
d) Perimeter: 10 cm — Area: 6 cm²
e) Perimeter: 16 cm — Area: 7 cm²

Challenge two

Lines drawn to join lengths as follows:

1 m – 100 cm	10 mm – 1 cm
80 cm – 0.8 m	5 m – 500 cm
1 km – 1,000 m	6 km – 6,000 m

Push yourself

Perimeter: 24 cm — Area: 15 cm²

Pages 30–31: 2D and 3D Shapes

Challenge one

a) Octagon **c)** 4 **e)** 6
b) 6 **d)** Circle

Challenge two

90 cm

Push yourself

Trapezium

Pages 32–33: Percentages

Challenge one

Percentage	Out of 100	How to find this %
1%	$\frac{1}{100}$	Divide the amount by 100
5%	$\frac{5}{100}$	Divide the amount by 20
10%	$\frac{10}{100}$	**Divide the amount by 10**
25%	$\frac{25}{100}$	**Divide the amount by 4**
50%	$\frac{50}{100}$	Divide the amount by 2
75%	$\frac{75}{100}$	**Divide the amount by 4 and multiply by 3**

Challenge two

White and red trainers (£21 compared to £24 for the white and black pair)

Push yourself

You can't have 5.5 children

Pages 34–35: Angles

Challenge one

(6 − 2) × 180° = 720°

Challenge two

Answers will vary.

Push yourself

$a = 80°$ $b = 310°$ $c = 96°$

Pages 36–37: Data Handling

Challenge one

Cricket   Tennis
Hockey   Golf
Football   Other
Basketball

Push yourself

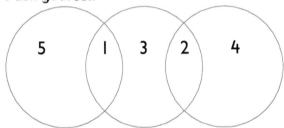

Pages 38–39: Averages

Challenge one

8 cars

Challenge two

15

Challenge three

23, 24, 25, 26, 27
If however, the street has odd numbers on one side
and even numbers on the other, they could be: 21, 23,
25, 27, 29

Push yourself

4, 4, 1

Pages 40–41: Fractions

Challenge one

$\frac{7}{14} + \frac{6}{14} = \frac{13}{14}$ (which can't be simplified)

Challenge two

45 metres

Push yourself

$\frac{1}{24}$ $\frac{2}{8}$ $\frac{8}{16}$ $\frac{3}{4}$ $\frac{20}{25}$

Pages 42–43: Compound Words

Challenge one

These are the compound words: airport; lighthouse;
doorbell; handshake; sunflower; driveway

Challenge two

Lines drawn to join words as follows:
tooth – brush   country – side

tip – toe   moon – light
chest – nut   under – ground
tea – cup   clock – wise
house – work
These words were included as a trick: no; kind; pole; your

Push yourself

Possible answers include:
backache; backbone; backdrop; backfire; background;
backhand; backlog; backpack; backseat; backstage;
backstop; backstroke; backtrack; backup; backwash;
backwater; backyard; comeback; cutback; feedback;
horseback; humpback; hunchback; hardback; outback;
paperback; setback; piggyback; tailback

Pages 44–45: Synonyms

Challenge one

Possible synonyms for 'small' include:
microscopic, minute, tiny, miniscule, miniature, mini,
little, compact
Possible synonyms for 'jump' include:
leap, bound, hop, bounce, dance, prance, frolic, bob

Challenge two

Answers will vary. Examples:
a) The <u>airy</u> room was <u>breezy</u> and <u>untidy</u>.
b) I <u>spotted</u> ships and yachts <u>bobbing</u> on the <u>tranquil</u>
    sea.
c) <u>Abruptly</u>, the <u>timber</u> door opened with a <u>clap</u>.
d) The <u>movie</u> was really <u>scary</u> and <u>enthralling</u>.

Push yourself

a) pushed   b) crept   c) cracked   d) decorated

Pages 46–47: Antonyms

Challenge one

Lines drawn to join the words as follows:
quick – slow   extend – shorten
doctor – patient   massive – minute
weak – sturdy

Fun fact

big, bulky, full-size, huge
petite, slight, little

Challenge two

a) **dis**pleasure b) **im**polite c) **un**able d) **un**likely

Push yourself

a) husband / **wife**   d) predator / **prey**
b) man / **woman**   e) off / **on**
c) dead / **alive**   f) buy / **sell**

Pages 48–49: Odd Two Out

Challenge one

Essex, Yorkshire, Cornwall, Hampshire
cow, doe, sow, mare
eagle, hawk, falcon, osprey
ruby, scarlet, crimson, red
lacrosse, squash, snooker, kabaddi

Challenge two

Answers will vary.

Push yourself

Answers will vary.

Pages 50–51: Double Letter Series

Challenge one

A	B	C	D	E	F	G	H	I	J	K	L	M
Z	Y	X	W	V	U	T	S	R	Q	P	O	N

EV is to GT as IR is to **KP**

All the pairs are mirrored letters but to solve the question you still need to consider the difference between the letters. First, 'E' to 'G' is two forwards and 'V' to 'T' is two backwards. Applying this to 'IR' gives the mirrored pair 'KP'.

Challenge two

Answers will vary.

Push yourself

Answers will vary.

Pages 52–53: Multiple Meanings

Challenge one

a) passage   c) coat   e) trunk

b) mean   d) brush   f) box

Challenge two

Lines drawn to join the words as follows:

chaos – havoc   wound – injury

change – amend   ample – plenty

benefit – gain   emerge – appear

contract – shrink   conclusion – end

hit – strike   edge – margin

Push yourself

Answers will vary. Examples:

address: the place where someone lives

address: a formal speech

badger: nocturnal mammal (grey and black coat)

badger: to pester somebody repeatedly

clip: fasten

clip: a flexible or spring-loaded device for holding an object

crane: a large, tall machine used for moving heavy objects

crane: stretch out one's body or neck in order to see something

date: the day of the month or year as specified by a number

date: a type of food

engaged: busy; occupied

engaged: having formally agreed to marry

fall: another word for the season of autumn

fall: an act of falling or collapsing

leaves: exits or departs

leaves: flattened structures of a plant, typically green and blade-like

Pages 54–55: Reshuffled Sentences

Challenge one

Lines drawn to join the words as follows:

Daniel – noun   school – noun

won – verb   chess – noun

the – determiner   tournament – noun

annual – adjective

Challenge two

a) Sweets and crisps aren't good for you.

b) Scarlet was late for her clarinet lesson.

c) Lots of people like cereal for breakfast.

Push yourself

a) garden   b) or   c) owns

Pages 56–57: Number Series

Challenge one

a) $7 \times 6 = 42$ d) $56 \div 7 = 8$

b) $19 - 6 = 13$ e) $24 + 23 = 47$

c) $(18 \div 3) + 6 = 12$ f) $(34 - 13) \div 7 = 3$

Challenge two

−16, −8, 8

Fun Fact

Add the previous two numbers to find the next number in the sequence.

Challenge three

Lines drawn to join the boxes as follows:

16, 25, 36, 49, 64, 81, 100, …   –   square numbers

53, 59, 61, 67, 71, 73, …   –   prime numbers

27, 64, 125, 216, 343, …   –   cube numbers

0, 1, 1, 2, 3, 5, 8, 13, 21, 34, 55, …   –   Fibonacci

Push yourself

The first, third, fifth numbers, etc. increase by 8 each time. The second, fourth, sixth numbers, etc. increase by 3 each time. The next number in the sequence is 56 (48 + 8).

Pages 58–59: Insert the Letter

Challenge one

Answers will vary. Example:

bathtub – bulb – blob – bib – bob – blurb – bomb

Challenge two

Answers will vary. Examples:

tr… – **tr**eat, **tr**uffle, **tr**ousers, **tr**iple, **tr**ibe, **tr**amp, **tr**ick, **tr**iumph

…lt – me**lt**, fe**lt**, be**lt**, vau**lt**, ma**lt**, sa**lt**, dea**lt**, ha**lt**

Push yourself

a) (length [**en**] sure)   (fast [**en**] emy)

b) (coa [**st**] age)   (moi [**st**] eer)

c) (cel [**lo**] cked)   (hel [**lo**] af)

Pages 60–61: Thinking Logically

Challenge one

Leah is 37

Challenge two

Buy the new Superclean bathroom cleaner! It'll leave your bathroom cleaner than any other! Superclean uses a mixture of soap and bleach that completely removes any sign of dust and grime. You won't be able to believe your eyes when you see what Superclean can do for you. Only £2.99 a bottle!

Push yourself

C Julian and Jun play rugby on Thursday.

Fun fact

186	187	188	189	190	191

Pages 62–63: Introduction to Non-Verbal Reasoning

Challenge one

From left to right, there are two fewer triangles in each figure.
So we are looking for a figure that has only two triangles. Therefore the answer is B.

Challenge two

Figure B has two more sides than Figure A.

Push yourself

Moving across the sequence from 1 to 4, the circle is moving from the left-hand side of the line, to the middle, to the right and then back to the left-hand side again. Did you spot the second part of the sequence? The circle is alternating between being transparent and not being transparent.

Pages 64–65: Odd One Out

Challenge one

In Figure B, the square in the final column of the third row is red compared to blue in Figure A.

Challenge two

Figure A is the odd one out. Figures B and C have one crossover, or intersection, but A does not.

Push yourself

C is the odd one out. It has an extra blue line on the right-hand side that the other figures don't have.

Pages 66–67: Series

Challenge one

From left to right, the circle moves to the end of the next line on the right.

Challenge two

The answer is B. There are the same number of blocks in each figure, but one more block is touching as you move from left to right in the series. Spot the 'red herring' in answer option A – there is indeed one more block touching, but not the same number of blocks overall, so it does not complete the series.

Push yourself

The answer is B. From left to right, each shape has one fewer side so the missing figure must have five sides. The shapes in the series are shaded black, so C cannot be correct.

Pages 68–69: Rotations

Challenge one

The answer is C.

Challenge two

The answer is C. Look at the stem – A and B are not a possible rotation. In both cases, the shape has been inverted and then rotated.

Push yourself

The answer is D.

Pages 70–71: Reflections

Challenge one

The answer is A. In B, the red shape has not been reflected and C has the wrong blue shape.

Challenge two

The answer is C. In A, the top triangle has not been reflected and in B the bottom of the shape has not been reflected properly.

Push yourself

The answer is E.

Pages 72–73: Matrices

Challenge one

The answer is B. Working down the left column, you can see that the shape has rotated by 90 degrees clockwise.

Challenge two

The answer is C. Moving across the rows from left to right, the figure in the right column is a reflection through the vertical axis of the figure in the left column.

Push yourself

The answer is B. Moving down each column, and across each row from the left, the number of sides on each shape reduces by one. So the missing figure must have five sides.

Pages 74–75: Analogies

Challenge one

The answer is B. The line in the original shape has no intersections. It is then changed into a line with one intersection. So we need to add one intersection to the 'test shape' in order to get the right answer. The test shape has two intersections, so the correct answer is B as it has three intersections.

Challenge two

The answer is C. The first figure is a stack of five coins and two coins are added to make it a stack of seven coins. The 'test figure' is a stack of eight coins so for the correct answer we are looking for a stack of ten coins.

Push yourself

The answer is E. In the first figure, the outlined shape becomes a shape with one extra side and black circles are added above and below. The test figure is an outlined pentagon (five sides), so we are looking for an answer which shows an outlined hexagon (six sides) with black circles added above and below. The answer is not B because black triangles have been added above and below the outlined hexagon.

Pages 76–77: Codes

Challenge one

The answer is C.
K = circles on left side, O = two circles

Challenge two

The answer is A.
B = pencils, D = one object

Push yourself

The answer is E.
C = wiggly arrow, D = arrow pointing to right

Pages 78–79: Hidden Shapes

Challenge one

The answer is C.

Challenge two

The answer is A.

Push yourself

The answer is E.

Pages 80–89: Mixed Activities

1 a) C   b) C   c) D
2 a) 169   b) 43   c) 32   d) 86
3 a) hope less   c) black bird
   b) clock wise
4 E
   All the others have four intersections.
5 a) question b) father   c) fight
6 Eight minutes past ten (o'clock)
   10:08 or 22:08
7 a) reject   decline
   b) deliberate   purposeful
   c) evaluation   assessment
8 A
   From left to right, the shape gains one side and moves to the next edge of the box, clockwise.
9 a) saddle   c) still   e) slow
   b) woman   d) trot

10 A shape with area 16 cm² and perimeter 16 cm

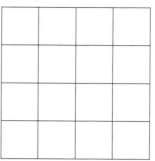

11 a) plural   singular
    b) continue   postpone
    c) ignorant   educated
12 E
13 a) station   b) train   c) wind   d) clouds
14 Hemisphere
15 a) cygnet   foal
    b) compact   microscopic
    c) eraser   sharpener
16 C
17 mouse; there; heads; nap
18 a) 2   c) £72   e) 200 m
    b) 200   d) 28 km
19 a) DW   b) IW   c) MN
20 B
    Moving down the columns, the number of circles in the top square multiplied by the number of circles in the middle square equals the number of circles in the bottom square.
21 a) large; black; winding   b) dog; path c) raced
22 a) 135°   b) North   c) South-East
23 a) note   b) trip   c) coat
24 C
    The top shape gains two sides and there is one fewer rounded rectangle.
25 Jack ran as fast as he could, and the ogre came rushing after, and **would** soon have caught him; only Jack had a start and dodged him a bit and **knew** where he was going. When he got to the beanstalk, the ogre was not more than twenty yards away when suddenly he **saw** Jack disappear like, and when he got up to the end of the **road** he saw Jack underneath **climbing** down for dear life.
26 a) January   b) March   c) 60 mm
27 a) yesterday   b) hopes   c) bowl
28 D
    K = dog facing down, O = no curved rectangle
29 a) B   b) D   c) C   d) A
30 20 kg
31 a) 10   b) 47   c) 122
32 C
33 a) e   b) w   c) l
34 a) 16   b) $\frac{19}{15}$ or $1\frac{4}{15}$ c) $\frac{4}{24}$
35 C